Ultimate Beginner's Guide to AI

*Practical Steps to Future-Proof Your Career,
Boost Productivity & Thrive in a
Rapidly Changing World of Innovation
(Even if You're not Tech-Savvy)*

MORGAN HALE

Ultimate Beginner's Guide to AI: Practical Steps to Future-Proof Your Career, Boost Productivity & Thrive in a Rapidly Changing World of Innovation (Even if You're not Tech-Savvy) by Morgan Hale

ISBN 978-1-7327551-8-5 (Trade Paperback)   ISBN 979-8-9987745-0-8 (Hardcover)

ISBN 978-1-7327551-9-2 (eBook)   ISBN 979-8-9987745-1-5 (Audiobook)

Library of Congress Control Number: 2025937595

Published by Tempered Books
An imprint of AD Books
Sheridan, Wyoming
adbooks.pub • info@adbooks.pub
permissions@adbooks.pub

Table of Contents

Note to Readers

This book includes examples of code, pseudocode, and system logic presented in two distinct formats:

1. **User Input** — Inline or brief single-line commands are presented in a monospace font like this: `calculate_forecast(data, model="exponential")`. These are intended to show individual inputs, functions, or expressions for reference or reuse.

2. **Code Blocks** — Longer, multi-line examples or scripts are set apart in dedicated blocks using a monospaced layout. These may represent a full process, configuration, or algorithm. For example:

```
def calculate_growth_rate(data):
cleaned = preprocess(data)
return model.predict(cleaned)
```

These blocks are designed to be easy to scan and understand in both print and digital formats.

Note: In order to preserve clarity across formats, line wrapping is minimized, and most code is written to fit within typical screen or page widths. If wrapping occurs, it should be interpreted as visual only—each code line should be read as independent unless otherwise noted.

For convenience, a digital copy of the code examples referenced throughout this book—along with the glossary and color text-to-image examples—can be accessed at the publisher's resource page:

adbooks.pub/resources

This resource is freely available to all readers and is designed to make applying the material in real-world scenarios easier, faster, and more practical. You may also access the web page by scanning this QR code.

Introduction
—
A Tale of Two Futures

K evin, a 45-year-old account manager, sat at his desk, staring at the email that had just popped up on his screen. The subject line screamed at him:

URGENT: AI Implementation in Sales Department.

As he read through the message, a knot formed in his stomach. The company was planning to integrate artificial intelligence (AI) into its processes, and all sales staff were expected to adapt and learn the new technology.

Kevin had two choices. He could ignore the email and hope that AI wouldn't impact his job. Or, he could embrace the change and learn how to work with AI. The first path, he realized, would likely lead to him becoming obsolete, possibly even losing his job to a younger, tech-savvy up-and-comer. The second path, while intimidating, could open up new opportunities and help him stay relevant in his field.

If Kevin's story sounds familiar, you're not alone. Many people today find themselves at a similar crossroads, unsure of how to navigate the rapidly changing world of AI. That's where this book comes in. Ultimate Beginner's Guide to AI is designed to demystify AI for beginners like you, providing

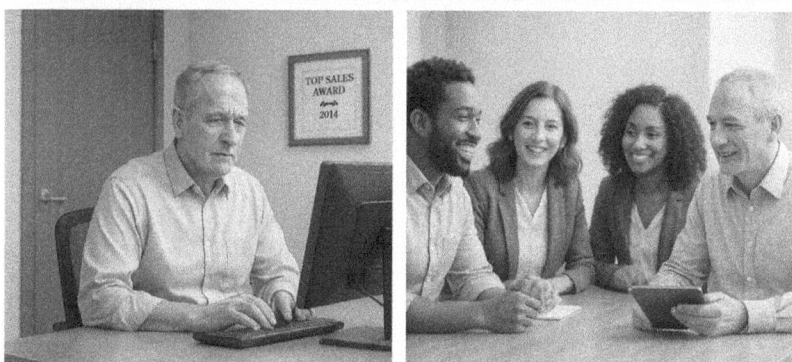

Which path will you choose?

practical steps and real-world examples to help you integrate AI into your personal and professional life. By the end of this book, you'll have the knowledge and confidence to embrace AI as an empowering tool rather than an intimidating subject.

You don't need to have prior technical knowledge to benefit from this book. Whether you're simply curious, looking to understand AI better, or you're a professional seeking to future-proof your career, this book is here to guide you every step of the way. You'll gain a foundational understanding of AI concepts, learn to use AI tools for work and play, and discover ways to enhance your productivity and stay ahead of the curve in your industry.

The book is structured to take you on a journey from basic AI concepts to practical applications and ethical considerations. Each chapter builds on the last to craft a comprehensive learning path that will transform the way you think about and interact with AI.

It's my intention to make AI accessible and understandable for everyone. With over three decades of experience as a mechanical engineer in the construction industry, I've witnessed firsthand how technology can disrupt entire professions. When computer-aided design (CAD) software first emerged, many drafters resisted the change, clinging to their pens and drawing boards. But those who adapted and learned to use CAD opened up new and exciting career opportunities for themselves.

Now, AI is knocking at our door, and it's up to us to decide how we'll respond. While AI hasn't yet taken over my job, I can see a pack of tech-savvy young engineers right behind me, ready to leverage the technology to work smarter and faster. That's why I embarked on my own AI journey—to stay relevant and competitive in my field.

But as I delved deeper into AI, I realized that its potential extends far beyond my own industry. I discovered it has the capability to transform our approach to problems, create new opportunities, and improve our overall quality of life. That's when I knew I had to share this knowledge with others, to help them not only survive but thrive in this new technological age.

Throughout this book, I encourage you to engage actively with the content, complete the exercises, and reflect on the real-world applications. Remember, learning to use AI is a journey that will enhance your personal and professional life in ways you might not even imagine.

So, let's embark on this AI journey together, with curiosity and open minds. By the time you finish this book, I hope you'll view AI as an empowering tool that can help you achieve more than you ever thought possible. Get ready to boost your productivity, future-proof your career, and thrive in a rapidly changing world of innovation.

Part 1
—
Fundamentals of AI

Chapter 1

—

What is AI? A Beginner's Overview

Y ou're standing in line at a coffee shop, and the person in front of you is chatting with a device in their ear. While this may seem ubiquitous on the surface, there's a catch. It's not a human on the other side of the conversation, but rather an AI assistant, helping with the day's schedule and offering recommendations on where to meet friends later.

This scene might have seemed like science fiction not long ago, but today, AI has seamlessly woven itself into our daily lives. Understanding AI is no longer optional. It's essential for thriving in our modern world. But what exactly is AI, and how did it come to be such an integral part of our lives?

AI Demystified

At it's core, artificial intelligence refers to the creation of machines that can mimic human-like cognitive functions such as learning, problem-solving, and decision-making. While these machines don't possess a mind or consciousness, they simulate intelligence by following complex sets of algorithms and data-processing techniques.

Think of AI as intelligent machines capable of performing jobs that typically require human insight. These tasks range widely, from voice recognition and language translation to data analysis and even playing chess. However, unlike humans, AI systems don't possess emotions, creativity, or ethical reasoning. They follow the logic and data they're given, performing with speed and precision.

When comparing AI to human intelligence, a fundamental distinction becomes clear. Human intelligence is characterized by creativity and the ability to navigate complex social dynamics. These traits arise from our capacity for abstract thinking, empathy, and consciousness, allowing us to adapt to new situations and express nuanced emotions. AI, on the other hand, excels in processing large amounts of data quickly and consistently, such as sorting through information or optimizing processes.

This difference is evident in the Turing Test, named for mathematician and computer scientist Alan Turing. The test measures how closely the machine's abilities resemble human intelligence. If a human can hold a conversation with a machine without realizing it's a machine, the test is passed. This test highlights AI's goal—not to replicate human consciousness but to simulate specific aspects of human thought and behavior.

In your everyday life, AI is often closer than you think. Consider virtual assistants like Siri, Alexa, or Google Assistant. Tools like these use natural language processing (NLP), a branch of AI that enables machines to understand and respond to human speech.

You might ask your assistant to update your calendar, queue your favorite playlist, or check the weather forecast. Behind the scenes, AI processes your request, interprets your command, and executes the action, all in the blink of an eye. These virtual assistants showcase AI's ability to integrate into our routines, making tasks more convenient and efficient.

Another everyday example is the recommendation algorithms used by streaming services like Netflix or Spotify. These algorithms analyze your viewing or listening habits to suggest new content you might enjoy. By identifying patterns in your behavior, AI curates a personalized experience tailored to your preferences. This ability to predict and adapt to user behavior demonstrates AI's potential to enhance our leisure activities, offering a customized experience that feels almost personal.

Moreover, AI tools like Grammarly and Canva Pro have redefined how we approach work and creativity. Grammarly makes use of AI to give real-time feedback on writing, correcting grammar and suggesting improvements in tone and style. It acts like an always-available editor, helping you communicate more effectively.

Canva Pro, on the other hand, employs AI to facilitate graphic design, offering tools that make crafting professional-looking visuals accessible to anyone, regardless of design expertise. These applications highlight AI's role in democratizing skills and empowering individuals to accomplish tasks with greater ease and proficiency.

As we explore AI further, remember that these intelligent machines are designed to support and enhance human capabilities, not replace them. AI and human intelligence complement each other, with AI providing data-driven insights while humans bring creativity and ethical judgment to the mix. This combination lets us address complicated problems more effectively, transforming challenges into opportunities.

As you continue learning about AI, consider how you can leverage these intelligent machines in your own life, enhancing productivity and opening new avenues for growth and innovation.

Common Misconceptions about AI

In the realm of AI, myths and misconceptions abound, often fueled by sensationalist media and dramatic science fiction. It's easy to get swept away by cinematic visions of AI, where machines become sentient and plot to dominate humanity. These portrayals, while entertaining, do little to educate us about the true nature and capabilities of AI.

To begin with, it's critical to differentiate between the robots we see in films and the AI systems we interact with daily. Movies often depict AI as humanoid robots with consciousness and emotions, whereas real-world AI consists of data-processing routines geared toward specific tasks. These systems lack self-awareness and emotions, operating instead on the instructions they're given, based on the data they've been trained on.

Another prevalent misconception is the idea that AI is poised to take over all human jobs, leaving us redundant and unemployed. While AI does automate certain tasks, it is more accurate to see it as a tool that augments human work rather than replacing it wholesale. AI excels in repetitive, data-driven tasks, freeing humans to focus on those jobs that require empathy, creativity, and nuanced decision-making.

A report by the World Economic Forum suggests that while AI may displace some jobs, it will also create new roles that we haven't yet imagined. For instance, while AI can efficiently analyze large sets of data in a medical context, the nuanced task of diagnosing patients and providing empathetic care remains in the hands of doctors. This collaborative dynamic enhances the quality of services without eliminating the need for human expertise.

Beyond these fears, there's often confusion about AI's limitations and capabilities. AI is not a wonder cure that can instantly solve all our problems. How well it works depends on the quality and quantity of data it processes. AI systems recognize patterns and then make decisions based on that data, but they cannot function beyond the scope of their programming.

For example, AI used in facial recognition can identify individuals in images with remarkable accuracy, but it struggles with tasks outside its specific design, such as understanding the context of a conversation. This specificity can be a strength, allowing AI to perform particular tasks with precision and speed, yet it underscores the importance of human oversight.

Let's address a specific example that highlights these limitations. Consider AI in the field of language translation. While AI can rapidly translate text between languages, it often struggles with context and nuance. Idiomatic expressions or cultural subtleties can lead to errors or misinterpretations. A phrase that makes perfect sense in one language might lose its meaning when translated literally into another. This limitation points back to the need for human input to ensure translations are not only accurate but also culturally appropriate.

Moreover, the idea that AI systems are impartial and unbiased is another myth. AI learns from the data it is fed, and if this data contains biases, the AI will likely perpetuate them. This bias is not a reflection of AI's failure but rather a reminder of the importance of human responsibility in curating balanced and fair datasets. Companies are increasingly aware of this, putting steps in place to recognize and address biases in AI systems. However, the myth of AI's objectivity persists, underscoring the need for ongoing education and ethical oversight.

It's worth noting that AI's speed and efficiency can also be seen as a limitation. While these attributes allow AI to process vast amounts of data quickly, they can lead to errors if the data is flawed or incomplete. For instance, in financial markets, AI algorithms can make split-second trading decisions based on data trends, but if the data is incorrect or manipulated, it can result in significant financial losses. This scenario illustrates the importance of human intervention in verifying data integrity and ensuring AI systems operate within safe parameters.

In summary, while AI is a powerful tool with the potential to transform industries and improve lives, it's not the omnipotent force often depicted in fiction. Understanding AI's true capabilities and limitations is crucial for leveraging its benefits while mitigating risks. By doing so, we can embrace AI as a partner in innovation rather than a looming threat.

Traditional Programming vs. Machine Learning

Imagine two chefs in a kitchen, each with their own way of preparing a meal. The first chef meticulously follows a recipe, measuring every ingredient and precisely adhering to each step. The second chef instead relies on tasting, tweaking as they go. This chef adjusts ingredients based on flavor, learning from each dish to improve the next.

These two approaches to cooking represent the key differences between traditional programming and machine learning. In traditional programming, operators write explicit instructions for computers to follow, providing detailed sets of rules in a defined sequence. These rules dictate how to process input data and produce the desired output. It's a linear process, much like following a recipe. Every possible scenario is accounted for in the code, and the computer executes these instructions without deviation.

The adaptive style of the second chef more closely resembles machine learning, a subset of AI where computers learn from data rather than relying solely on predefined rules. Machine learning systems are designed to identify patterns and make decisions based on data input. They don't require explicit instructions for every possible scenario. Instead, they learn from examples and adjust their behavior accordingly. This adaptability allows machine learning models to handle complex tasks where traditional programming might falter.

Machine learning's data-driven approach offers several advantages. It can handle tasks that are too complex for rule-based programming. However, it also presents challenges. Machine learning models require huge amounts of data to learn effectively, and their performance can be affected by the quality of this data. Moreover, the process of training a model can be less predictable than traditional programming. It's an iterative process involving experimentation and adjustment to improve accuracy.

Yet, this flexibility allows machine learning to adapt to new information without the need for constant manual updates. In a world where data is

Traditional Programming: Input → Decision → Process → Output

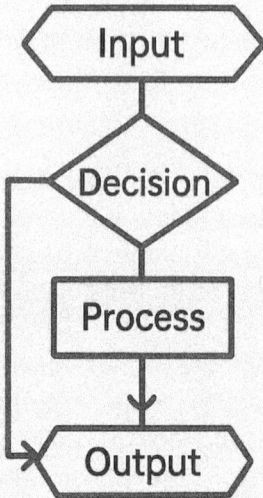

Neural Network: Input, Output

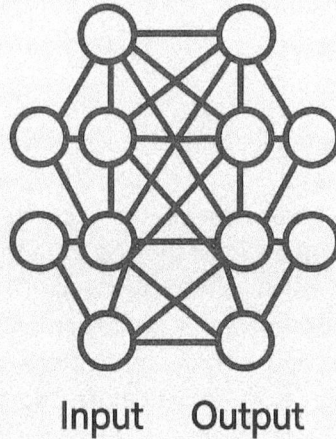

constantly evolving, this adaptability is invaluable. For instance, consider self-driving cars. They rely on machine learning models to interpret data from sensors and cameras, making split-second decisions in dynamic environments. Traditional programming would struggle to account for every possible driving scenario, but machine learning can adapt to new situations based on what it has learned from past experiences.

In summary, traditional programming and machine learning offer different approaches to solving problems. Traditional programming provides precision and predictability, making it ideal for tasks with clear, defined rules. Machine learning, with its data-driven adaptability, excels in handling complexity and variability. As you explore AI, understanding these differences will help you appreciate the diverse ways technology can be applied to address challenges and innovate in our ever-changing world.

Key Takeaways

- AI simulates specific human-like cognitive functions (like learning, problem-solving, and decision-making), but it does not possess consciousness, emotions, or self-awareness.

- Everyday examples of AI include virtual assistants (Siri, Alexa), recommendation systems (Netflix, Spotify), and productivity tools (Grammarly, Canva Pro), illustrating its integration into daily life.

- AI is a tool, not a replacement—it complements human strengths, enabling people to focus on creativity, empathy, and complex decision-making.

- Common myths—like AI being sentient or destined to take over all jobs—are rooted in fiction. Real-world AI is task-specific, data-dependent, and lacks autonomy.

- Bias and data quality affect AI performance, showing that AI is not inherently objective or perfect—human oversight remains essential.

- Traditional programming vs. machine learning highlights two key paradigms: rule-based logic versus pattern recognition and adaptability.

Chapter 2

—

AI at Home

N ot long ago, a responsive home that adjusted itself to your preferences felt like the stuff of sci-fi.

Now, with just a step inside, the lights shift, the temperature adjusts, and your favorite music begins to play—no buttons pressed.

This isn't futuristic fantasy—it's the new normal in AI-powered living, where convenience meets deep personalization and changes how we engage with our environments.

Exploring Smart Home Devices

Smart speakers, such as Amazon Echo and Google Home, have become the cornerstone of modern smart homes. These devices are powered by AI and act as virtual assistants, ready to cater to your every need. Imagine you're in the kitchen, hands deep in flour while baking, and you suddenly need to convert measurements. All it takes is a voice command to your smart speaker, and you'll have the answer without missing a beat.

These speakers can do much more than answer questions, though. They can control other smart devices in your home, allowing you to dim the lights or lock the doors with just your voice. This seamless integration of AI into daily life enhances convenience, making mundane tasks feel effortless.

Another marvel of AI in the home is the AI-enabled thermostat, epitomized by devices like the Nest Learning Thermostat. Not only do these smart thermostats regulate temperature, but they learn from your habits. Over time, they adjust heating and cooling schedules based on your preferences and routines. Imagine waking up in the morning to a perfectly warm house in winter, without having to adjust the thermostat manually.

These devices also contribute to energy efficiency, learning when you leave for work and adjusting the temperature to save energy while you're away. By reducing energy waste, smart thermostats can reduce the money you spend on utilities, and at the same time contribute to a more sustainable lifestyle.

Smart lighting systems have also transformed home environments, offering both aesthetic and practical benefits. With systems like Philips Hue, you can change both the color and brightness of your lights through an app or voice command.

Ready for movie night? Or maybe you're hosting a party. Now, you can set the perfect ambiance for any occasion, all with a voice command or a tap on your smartphone. These systems can adjust automatically based on the time of day or your schedule, ensuring that your lighting is always just right. Moreover, smart lighting can enhance security by simulating your presence when you're away, deterring potential intruders.

These advanced AI-powered devices aren't just about convenience. They're about creating a more harmonious living environment. They offer a level of control and customization that allows you to tailor your home to your lifestyle needs.

As you interact with these devices, you'll notice how they anticipate your preferences, making your home not just smarter, but more in tune with you. This technology empowers you to focus on what truly matters, freeing up time and energy for the things you love.

As you integrate these smart devices into your home, you'll find them becoming indispensable allies in managing your day-to-day life. They represent a new era where technology doesn't just serve us. It understands us.

By embracing these innovations, you can enhance your quality of life, making your living space a true reflection of your needs and desires. The smart home revolution is here, and it's making life better in ways we could only dream of a decade ago.

AI's Impact on Daily Routines

Instead of being jolted out of sleep by a screaming alarm clock, wouldn't it be nice to awaken to the soft glow of lights slowly brightening, simulating a sunrise, while your favorite morning playlist gently fills the room. Meanwhile, the scent of freshly brewed coffee wafts from the kitchen, all without you lifting a finger.

These are not just perks of a futuristic home but realities of today, thanks to AI's transformative impact on our daily routines. The beauty of AI lies in its ability to streamline household tasks, making everyday life not only more convenient but also more efficient.

Whether schedule-based or on the fly, with a simple command you can adjust the lights, play music, or even preheat your oven. This hands-free convenience means that while you're busy with one task, you can simultaneously manage another. This capability turns multitasking into a seamless experience, freeing up your hands and mind to focus on what truly matters. The ease and immediacy of voice commands allow you to interact with technology in a natural, intuitive way, bridging the gap between you and your devices.

Automation takes this convenience a step further by anticipating your needs before you even express them. AI-enabled systems can learn your routines and preferences, automating tasks to suit your lifestyle. The ability to schedule devices to turn on and off or adjust settings at specific times adds even more efficiency, allowing you to optimize energy use without a second thought.

Beyond individual tasks, AI's integration into our routines fosters a more connected and harmonious living environment. It allows different devices to communicate with each other, creating a cohesive network of smart technology. Your alarm clock can tell your coffee maker to start brewing as soon as you hit snooze. Your smart fridge can alert you when you're running low on groceries and suggest a shopping list. This interconnected ecosystem of devices enhances the overall functionality of your home, making it responsive to your daily needs.

The impact of AI on daily routines extends beyond the home. It influences how we manage our time, work, and leisure activities, creating a more balanced lifestyle. With AI handling repetitive tasks, you have more time to spend on activities that bring you joy or contribute to personal growth. Whether it's reading a book, going for a walk, or pursuing a hobby, AI's support allows you to prioritize what truly matters.

AI's role in daily routines also highlights the power of personalization. As these systems learn your habits and preferences, they tailor their responses to suit your unique lifestyle. This personalization transforms technology from a tool into a companion that understands you and adapts to your needs. By continuously learning and evolving, AI offers an ever-improving experience that aligns with your goals and aspirations.

As you navigate the integration of AI into your routines, consider the possibilities it opens up. The convenience and efficiency AI brings to daily life are just the beginning. The potential for innovation and enhancement is limited only by your imagination and willingness to embrace change. With AI as an ally, you stand on the cusp of a new era where technology enriches every aspect of your life, making the ordinary extraordinary.

Popular Apps Powered by AI

In our daily digital interactions, AI quietly enhances our experiences, often without us even realizing it. Consider social media platforms, a space where AI plays a significant role in shaping what we see.

Platforms like Facebook use sophisticated algorithms to curate content, aiming to show you posts, ads, and updates that align with your interests. This curation is driven by AI analyzing your interactions—what you like, share, or comment on—to predict what content will keep you engaged. It's this tailored experience that keeps users scrolling, creating a personalized feed that feels uniquely yours.

Behind the scenes, AI is assessing vast amounts of data in real time, learning from your behavior to refine its predictions. This process not only keeps the platform engaging but also maximizes the time users spend interacting with content.

Streaming services like Netflix also utilize AI to enhance user experience. When you browse through Netflix's library, the recommendations you receive are not random. AI algorithms analyze your viewing history, genres, and even how much time you spend watching certain types of content to suggest shows and movies that match your tastes. This personalized recommendation system is why you might discover a new series that perfectly fits your mood or stumble upon a film you never knew you wanted to watch.

The AI learns from each interaction, becoming more attuned to your preferences over time. This constant learning loop creates a streaming experience that feels both intuitive and personal, offering content that matches your interests and viewing habits.

Navigation apps like Google Maps have transformed how we navigate our world, and AI is at the heart of this transformation. When you use Google Maps to find the quickest route to your destination, AI is hard at work, analyzing real-time traffic data, historical traffic patterns, and user reports to provide accurate and efficient directions. This dynamic traffic prediction allows the app to suggest alternative routes when delays are detected, helping you avoid the heaviest traffic and reach your destination faster.

The accuracy and efficiency of these predictions rely on AI's ability to process and interpret massive datasets, turning complex information into actionable guidance. Whether you're commuting to work or exploring a new city, AI ensures that your journey is as smooth and stress-free as possible.

AI's influence even extends to online shopping platforms like Amazon, where recommendation engines suggest products based on your browsing and purchase history. These suggestions are driven by AI analyzing patterns in your shopping behavior, allowing the platform to offer relevant and appealing products. This tailored shopping experience not only makes the process more convenient but also increases the likelihood of you finding exactly what you're looking for, often before you even realize you want it. The result is a shopping journey that feels intuitive and efficient, with AI guiding you to products that suit your needs and preferences.

These AI-powered apps have become integral to how we interact with technology, shaping our experiences in subtle yet profound ways. By learning from our behaviors and preferences, AI creates a world where our digital interactions are more personalized, efficient, and enjoyable.

Whether it's through content curation, personalized recommendations, or dynamic navigation, AI enhances our daily routines, making technology feel less like a tool and more like an extension of ourselves.

Facilitating Daily Tasks

You've awakened to a simulated sunrise and enjoyed your freshly brewed coffee. As your morning unfolds, your AI digital companion is now ready to streamline routine tasks, making them almost invisible.

Virtual assistants like Siri and Google Assistant have become indispensable allies in managing daily life. They do more than just respond to questions. They anticipate your needs and adapt to your lifestyle. Picture yourself juggling a busy morning, and with a simple voice command, your assistant sends a text, reminds you of a meeting, and sets a timer for your breakfast eggs.

These tasks, once requiring individual attention, are now seamlessly integrated into your routine, freeing you to focus on more significant matters. The ease of delegating mundane tasks to AI allows you to reclaim moments for creativity and reflection, a luxury in today's fast-paced world.

While virtual assistants can handle scheduling, answer questions, and set reminders, their capabilities extend far beyond these basic functions. They learn from your habits, offering suggestions that align with your preferences.

If you've been searching for a new recipe, your assistant might recommend a popular dish based on your previous searches or even help compile a shopping list. This ability to personalize interactions turns a simple tool into a powerful extension of your daily routine. By understanding your patterns, virtual assistants help create a more efficient and harmonious lifestyle, reducing the cognitive load of managing multiple tasks.

Expense tracking and budgeting apps offer another layer of convenience in managing daily life, leveraging AI analytics to simplify financial tasks. These apps go beyond simply balancing your checkbook. They provide insights into your spending habits, helping you make informed financial decisions.

Imagine an app that automatically categorizes your expenses, alerts you to unusual spending, and even suggests areas where you might save. These intelligent systems analyze your financial data, offering a clearer picture of your financial health. By identifying patterns and trends, they empower you to take control of your finances, promoting a sense of stability and security in an often unpredictable world.

The power of AI in these apps lies in their ability to learn from your behavior, offering tailored advice that resonates with your financial goals. Whether it's saving for a vacation, paying off debt, or simply managing monthly expenses, these apps provide a roadmap to financial well-being. They remove the guesswork from budgeting, presenting data in a way that's easy to understand and act upon. This clarity turns financial management from a daunting task into an achievable goal, enhancing your confidence in navigating personal finance.

AI-driven tools have become integral to our daily lives, subtly transforming how we manage time, tasks, and finances. These innovations offer more than convenience. They empower us to live more fulfilling lives.

Key Takeaways

- AI integrates seamlessly into routines by learning from your habits, allowing automation of daily tasks such as temperature adjustment, lighting schedules, or grocery management.

- Popular apps like Netflix, Google Maps, and Amazon use AI to provide tailored recommendations, real-time navigation, and curated experiences based on user behavior.

- Voice assistants (Siri, Alexa, Google Assistant) act as AI companions, helping with reminders, texts, shopping lists, and more, learning from usage to improve over time.

- AI enhances financial management through budgeting and expense tracking apps that analyze your habits, flag anomalies, and suggest improvements.

- The core value of AI in daily life isn't just automation—it's freeing up your time and mental space to focus on what matters most.

Chapter 3

—

Enhancing Personal Productivity with AI

T ime is one of our most precious resources—and AI is transforming how we spend it.

From scheduling meetings to drafting emails, intelligent tools are reshaping our productivity routines. Whether you're launching a startup or organizing your daily to-dos, these systems are designed to adapt to your needs, helping you focus where it matters most.

AI-Powered Productivity

AI-driven task managers and schedulers are at the forefront of this transformation. Tools like Motion and Notion have become indispensable for individuals and teams alike. Motion integrates seamlessly with your calendar, optimizing your day by automatically scheduling tasks based on deadlines and priorities. This digital assistant not only reminds you of upcoming meetings, but also suggests the best times to tackle specific tasks, helping you stay on track.

Such proactive scheduling minimizes downtime and helps maintain focus, allowing you to allocate your energy efficiently throughout the day.

These tools learn from your habits, adapting to your workflow and making real-time adjustments to accommodate changes, whether it's a sudden meeting or a last-minute deadline.

In addition to scheduling, AI-generated reminders and alerts provide powerful tools for managing your time effectively. Picture an AI assistant that anticipates your needs, sending gentle nudges to keep you organized and on target. These reminders go beyond simple notifications. They're tailored to your preferences, learning when and how you best respond to prompts.

Whether it's reminding you to take a break, follow up on an email, or prepare for an upcoming presentation, your alerts are designed to enhance productivity without overwhelming you. By taking over the task of managing multiple reminders, AI allows you to focus on the task at hand, fostering an environment where productivity flourishes.

Note-taking apps with AI organization features, such as Notion, bring a new level of efficiency to capturing and retrieving information. Gone are the days of sifting through disorganized notes scattered across various platforms. With AI-powered tools, your notes not only become more accessible but also more intelligent. These apps categorize and tag content, making it easy to find relevant information when you need it.

Imagine jotting down ideas during a brainstorming session and having AI organize them into coherent themes, ready to be expanded upon later. This level of organization ensures that no idea gets lost in the shuffle, enabling you to harness the full potential of your creativity and insights.

The integration of AI into these productivity tools is not just about convenience. It's about creating a seamless experience that aligns with your personal and professional goals. This shift not only enhances productivity but also contributes to a sense of fulfillment and balance in your daily life.

As you embrace these tools, you'll find that they not only save you time but also enable you to make more informed choices, ultimately leading to increased effectiveness and satisfaction in your endeavors.

Facilitating Creative Processes

How many times have you sat at your desk, ready to start a new project, and been daunted by the dreaded blank page or empty canvas? The pressure to come up with original ideas can be overwhelming. This is where AI steps in as a creative ally, providing the tools and inspiration to transform your concepts into reality.

In the area of graphic design, AI-powered tools have revolutionized the creative process, making it more accessible and dynamic. Tools like Canva and Adobe Sensei use machine learning algorithms to assist in generating design elements, offering suggestions that enhance your projects with minimal effort. Whether you're a seasoned designer or a novice, AI facilitates the exploration of new styles and techniques, pushing the boundaries of creativity.

Consider Canva, a versatile platform that democratizes design. It offers a broad array of templates and design suggestions powered by AI, streamlining the creative workflow. You no longer need to start from scratch or worry about matching colors and fonts. Instead, AI analyzes your design choices, suggesting complementary elements that ensure your work is cohesive and visually appealing.

This level of guidance not only speeds up the design process but also empowers users to experiment with confidence, knowing that AI is there to support their artistic vision. For those with limited design experience, Canva provides an invaluable resource, opening doors to creativity that might have previously been closed.

Adobe Sensei takes this a step further by weaving AI into its suite of creativity tools. It offers features such as content-aware fill and auto-tagging, which simplify complex design tasks. When refining an image, Sensei can intelligently remove unwanted elements and adjust lighting to enhance the overall composition. This capability allows you to focus on the creative aspects of your project, reducing the time spent on technical adjustments. The fusion of AI and design software results in an intuitive experience that encourages creativity without sacrificing quality or precision.

Writing, too, benefits from AI's creative capabilities. The act of crafting a compelling narrative or article often involves multiple drafts and revisions. AI writing assistants are transforming how writers approach this process, offering real-time suggestions that improve clarity, grammar, and style. Your digital writing companion can review your text, highlight areas for improvement, and suggest alternative phrasing that better captures your intended message. This feedback loop fosters a more efficient writing process, enabling you to produce polished content with ease.

Tools like Grammarly and Hemingway App provide valuable insights into your writing, targeting common pitfalls such as passive voice or complex sentence structures. These AI-driven platforms analyze your text, offering suggestions that enhance readability and engagement.

Whether you're drafting an email or composing a novel, AI writing assistants streamline the editing process, ensuring your work resonates with your audience. The ability to receive instant feedback encourages experimentation and refinement, resulting in a more compelling narrative.

Moreover, AI can serve as a brainstorming partner, offering inspiration when creative blocks arise. Imagine feeding a few keywords or concepts into an AI tool, which then generates a web of related ideas and themes. This process sparks new avenues for exploration, breaking through the barriers of conventional thinking. AI's ability to assess and synthesize vast amounts of information quickly provides a fresh perspective, invigorating your creative projects with innovative ideas.

In the world of content creation, AI's impact is profound. It not only assists in the technical aspects of design and writing but also nurtures the creative spirit, encouraging users to push their boundaries. By automating routine tasks and offering helpful suggestions, AI frees you to express your unique voice and vision. As you embrace these tools, you'll find yourself exploring new dimensions of creativity, empowered by the synergy between human ingenuity and artificial intelligence.

Integrating AI into Daily Routines

We've all had those days when there are too many tasks to wrap your arms around and not enough daylight to get them all done. An AI-powered, personalized productivity dashboard is one way to tackle this challenge.

Picture a digital command center tailored to your unique needs, where every tool and piece of information is at your fingertips. Such dashboards use AI to consolidate data from various sources, presenting it in a cohesive format that maximizes efficiency. Whether you're managing work, personal projects, or household chores, having everything in one place streamlines your workflow and reduces the mental clutter that often accompanies a busy day.

Creating a personalized productivity dashboard starts with identifying your key priorities. What tasks need regular attention? Which projects are ongoing? What deadlines loom on the horizon? By determining these elements, you can configure your dashboard to reflect what's important, ensuring that nothing falls through the cracks. AI enhances this process by learning from your interactions, suggesting adjustments and improvements over time.

For instance, if you're consistently overlooking a particular task, the system might recommend highlighting it or changing its priority. This dynamic adaptability means your dashboard evolves alongside your needs, always offering the most relevant information and tools.

Incorporating AI tools into your daily routine isn't just about organization. It's about optimizing performance. Regular updates to AI applications are crucial to maintaining their effectiveness. Technology changes quickly, and keeping up with the latest features and improvements ensures you're benefiting from the most advanced capabilities.

Updates often include enhancements to speed, functionality, and security, making your tools more reliable and efficient. By setting aside time to review and apply updates, you ensure that your AI-assisted productivity remains at its peak, allowing you to focus on tasks that matter without worrying about technical hiccups.

To stay current with AI updates, consider enabling automatic updates where possible. This feature ensures that your tools are consistently refreshed with the latest advancements without requiring manual intervention. Additionally, staying informed about new features and changes allows you to leverage improvements to your routine.

For example, an updated AI scheduling tool might offer new integration options with other apps you use, broadening its utility and effectiveness. By keeping your tools optimized, you're not only enhancing performance but also ensuring a smoother, more seamless experience that supports your day-to-day activities.

Beyond performance, integrating AI into your routine involves a mindset shift toward embracing technology as a partner rather than a tool. This shift means being open to experimenting with different approaches, allowing AI to suggest new ways to tackle tasks and solve problems.

As AI learns from your habits and preferences, it offers insights that can change how you approach your work and personal projects. Your AI assistant can analyze your productivity patterns, identifying peak times for creativity or focus. With this information, you can schedule tasks that align with your natural rhythms, maximizing output and minimizing fatigue.

Moreover, integrating AI into your routine fosters a mindset of continuous improvement. As you become more familiar with how AI can enhance your productivity, you'll likely discover new applications and opportunities for innovation. Whether it's streamlining communication, automating repetitive tasks, or exploring creative pursuits, AI opens doors to possibilities you might not have considered. This ongoing exploration encourages growth and adaptability, equipping you with the tools and mindset needed to navigate an ever-evolving landscape.

As you explore the integration of AI into your daily life, remember that your goal is not perfection but progress. Each small step toward incorporating AI tools brings you closer to a more organized, efficient, and fulfilling routine. The process is iterative, with room for experimentation and adjustment as you discover what works best for you.

By embracing AI's potential, you're not just enhancing your productivity—you're paving the way for a future where technology complements and enhances your capabilities in meaningful ways.

Key Takeaways

- Smart reminders and note-taking apps reduce mental load by anticipating user needs, organizing information, and suggesting optimal timing for tasks.

- Creative tools like Canva, Adobe Sensei, Grammarly, and Hemingway App harness AI to support design, writing, and brainstorming—enabling users to produce polished, compelling content more easily.

- AI-enhanced dashboards consolidate information and tasks, adapt to user priorities, and evolve over time to reflect changes in routine and workload.

- Adopting AI as a partner rather than a passive tool encourages ongoing experimentation, self-awareness, and increased productivity aligned with individual rhythms and goals.

Chapter 4

—

Navigating the Ethics of AI

A job interview takes place. You're ready for questions—only this time, you're also being assessed by an AI. It reviews your words, gestures, and even facial expressions, all while drawing on data that might carry hidden biases.

This isn't a hypothetical. It's a reality many are already facing. As AI systems gain influence over critical decisions, understanding the ethical stakes becomes more urgent than ever.

Hidden Bias in AI

AI bias refers to the prejudices that can be embedded within AI systems, stemming from the data used to train them. At its core, AI functions by processing large datasets to identify patterns and make decisions. However, if the data contains biases, the AI will inevitably replicate these biases, resulting in skewed outcomes.

For instance, an AI model trained predominantly on data from a single demographic could fail to accurately represent or serve other demographics.

This is because AI, despite its complexity, can't discern context beyond the data it is given. It learns "what is" rather than "what ought to be." This can perpetuate existing inequalities rather than rectify them.

Some examples of AI bias can highlight its real-world consequences. Consider the case of a healthcare algorithm in the United States that was designed to allocate resources to patients. This algorithm inadvertently favored white patients over black patients. The bias arose because the algorithm used historical data from healthcare costs as a proxy for health needs, not accounting for systemic disparities in healthcare access and spending among different racial groups.

Similarly, the COMPAS algorithm, used in US courts to predict recidivism, was found to predict higher rates of false positives for black offenders compared to white offenders. This skewed outcome resulted in unfair sentencing, highlighting the severe implications of biased AI decision-making tools in the justice system.

Another striking example is Amazon's hiring algorithm, which showed bias against women. The algorithm was trained on resumes submitted over the past ten years, a period during which the tech industry was male-dominated. Consequently, the AI favored male candidates, perpetuating gender disparity in hiring practices.

Such cases highlight the crucial need for vigilance and corrective measures in AI development to ensure fairness and equality. Addressing AI bias requires a multifaceted approach.

One effective strategy is to ensure that training data reflects diverse and representative samples. By doing so, AI systems can learn to recognize and accommodate a broader spectrum of human experiences and characteristics. This involves actively sourcing data that includes underrepresented groups and contexts, thereby reducing the likelihood of bias. Additionally, implementing robust data governance practices can help monitor and evaluate data for potential biases before it is used in training AI models.

Model evaluation by diverse social groups is another crucial step in mitigating AI bias. Involving individuals from various backgrounds in the testing phase can provide valuable insights into how AI systems perform across different demographics. This collaborative approach helps identify and rectify bias that might not be readily apparent to developers. Moreover, periodic audits of AI systems can ensure they remain fair and effective over time, adapting to changes in society and technology.

Finally, fostering a culture of accountability within organizations developing and deploying AI is essential. This involves creating ethical guidelines and frameworks that prioritize fairness and transparency. By holding AI systems accountable for their outcomes, developers and organizations can work towards more equitable and just applications of AI technology. These measures, combined with ongoing research and innovation, pave the way for AI systems that not only perform efficiently but also uphold ethical standards.

Privacy Concerns in the Age of AI

Picture a world where your every move, purchase, and conversation is monitored and analyzed by AI systems. This isn't some dystopian vision of a distant future. It's a reality we're grappling with today.

AI technologies, while offering incredible benefits, also pose significant threats to individual privacy. These systems collect large volumes of data to function effectively, from your browsing habits to location information. This data doesn't just include numbers or figures. It forms a comprehensive map of your personal and professional life, offering glimpses into your preferences, behaviors, and even your personality. This level of surveillance, while often subtle, raises profound questions about how much of our privacy we're willing to sacrifice for convenience.

The implications for society are vast. As AI systems become more integrated into our daily routines, the boundary between public and private life blurs. Smart home devices like virtual assistants constantly listen for commands, meaning they also capture ambient conversations.

AI-driven advertising platforms track your online behavior to tailor ads specifically to your interests. While these technologies can enhance user experience, they also create detailed profiles that can be exploited if mismanaged.

The potential for misuse is not limited to commercial interests. Governments and other entities could also access this data, leading to surveillance that infringes upon civil liberties. As AI evolves, the challenge lies in balancing innovation with the protection of individual rights.

To address these concerns, governments have enacted laws to safeguard personal data and ensure privacy. Two of the most influential regulations are the European Union's General Data Protection Regulation (GDPR) and the California Consumer Privacy Act (CCPA). These laws establish the framework for how businesses can collect, store, and use personal data.

The CCPA, applicable to businesses handling data from California residents, grants consumers rights such as accessing their data, requesting its deletion, and opting out of data sales. This regulation aims to give individuals more control over their personal information, promoting transparency in how businesses operate.

The GDPR provides even stricter guidelines, requiring businesses to obtain the user's explicit consent before processing their personal data. It grants individuals the right to access their data, rectify inaccuracies, and even transfer their information to other service providers. One of the most significant aspects of GDPR is its emphasis on the user's right to be forgotten, allowing them to request their personal data erased under certain conditions.

These regulations not only protect personal privacy but also hold organizations accountable for the unethical use of AI and data-driven technologies. However, compliance can be complex, especially as different jurisdictions introduce their own variations of privacy laws.

Despite these protections, the responsibility ultimately falls on users to manage their data actively. There are several ways individuals can maintain control over their information in AI interactions.

First, understanding privacy settings on devices and platforms is crucial. Many services offer customizable privacy options, allowing users to limit data collection and sharing. Taking the time to review and adjust these settings can significantly reduce exposure to unwanted data gathering. Additionally, being aware of the permissions given to apps and devices can prevent unnecessary data access.

Another effective strategy is using privacy-focused tools and technologies. Virtual private networks (VPNs) can obscure online activity, making it harder for third parties to track browsing habits. Similarly, encrypted messaging apps ensure that communications remain private, accessible only to the intended recipients.

By adding these tools into their daily routines, users can enhance their privacy without compromising the benefits of AI technologies. Furthermore, keeping abreast of the latest developments in AI and data privacy can empower individuals to make better decisions about how their data is used.

Education and awareness are vital components in the fight for privacy. As AI technologies advance, so too must our understanding of their implications. By recognizing the potential privacy risks, and then taking deliberate steps to mitigate them, individuals can navigate the digital landscape more safely. Engaging with resources and communities dedicated to data privacy can provide valuable insights and support, fostering a culture of vigilance and empowerment.

In the broader context, privacy in the age of AI is not just a personal concern but a societal one. As users, developers, and policymakers work together to address these challenges, the goal should be to create a future where technology and privacy can work in harmony with one another. This balance is essential for ensuring that AI is used as a means of empowerment rather than a tool for control.

The journey toward a more privacy-conscious society involves collaboration and commitment from all stakeholders, with the understanding that privacy is a fundamental right worth protecting.

Transparency in AI: Understanding the Black Box

Imagine trying to work out the inner functionality of a complex machine, only to be faced with a sealed box that offers no insight into how it functions. This captures the essence of AI's "black box" problem, a situation where even the developers of AI systems struggle to explain how decisions are made. The complexity of these systems, especially those using deep learning, often renders them opaque.

This lack of clarity creates significant challenges for accountability, as it becomes difficult to pinpoint errors or biases in the decision-making process. Users, understandably, may find it hard to trust AI when its reasoning remains a mystery. For AI to truly be an asset to society, it must operate transparently, allowing users to understand and trust the outcomes it produces.

The first step in addressing the black box problem is to enhance the interpretability of AI systems. Interpretability refers to the ease of explaining how an AI model arrives at a particular decision. By making models more interpretable, developers can provide insights into the decision-making process.

One approach involves using simpler models, such as decision trees or linear regression, which are inherently more transparent. While these models may not capture the complexity of deep learning networks, they offer a clearer view of how inputs are transformed into outputs.

Another strategy is to employ techniques that explain complex models. For example, saliency maps highlight the parts of an input (like an image) that most influence the AI's decision, offering a visual explanation of the model's focus. These methods, though not perfect, provide valuable windows into the AI's internal logic.

Increased transparency is crucial for fostering trust between users and AI systems. When users understand how AI arrives at decisions, they are more likely to trust and accept its output. Transparency also empowers users to identify and challenge unfair or biased decisions, promoting fairness and accountability.

In contexts like healthcare or finance, where AI-driven decisions can have profound impacts on life and livelihood, transparency ensures that stakeholders can scrutinize and validate the processes involved. This scrutiny is essential for preventing discrimination and ensuring that AI systems uphold ethical standards.

Moreover, transparency supports accountability by clarifying the responsibilities of AI developers and users. When decision-making processes are transparent, it becomes easier to assign responsibility for errors or biases. Developers can identify flaws in their models and implement corrective measures, while users can make informed choices regarding their interactions with AI systems. This mutual understanding fosters a culture of accountability, where all parties recognize their roles in ensuring ethical AI use. Organizations, too, benefit from transparency, as it helps them meet regulatory requirements and build trust with consumers.

Explainable AI (XAI) is an emerging field with the goal of enhancing transparency in AI systems. XAI focuses on creating models that offer clear, understandable explanations of their decisions. By offering users insights into how AI processes information, XAI bridges the gap between complex algorithms and human comprehension.

This field is critical for regulatory compliance, as many laws now require AI systems to be explainable. For instance, the European Union's GDPR states that individuals have the right to understand the logic behind automated decisions that affect them. By adopting XAI principles, organizations can meet these requirements while fostering user trust.

The development of explainable AI models involves a multidisciplinary approach, combining insights from computer science, psychology, and human-computer interaction. This collaboration ensures that explanations are not only accurate but also meaningful to users. For example, researchers might study how people interpret visual explanations to design more intuitive interfaces. This user-centered approach ensures that XAI systems align with human cognitive processes, making AI more accessible and understandable.

As AI systems become more autonomous and integrated into critical decision-making, the demand for transparency and accountability will only grow. Organizations must invest in XAI research and development, testing their models to ensure that they align with societal values. Engaging with stakeholders, including users and regulators, is vital for creating AI systems that reflect diverse perspectives and address ethical concerns. By prioritizing transparency, developers can build AI systems that not only excel in performance but also earn the trust and acceptance of users.

In conclusion, transparency in AI is not merely a technical challenge but a fundamental requirement of ethical AI deployment. By understanding and addressing the black box problem, we can develop systems that are both powerful and responsible. Transparent AI systems foster user trust, support accountability, and ensure that AI serves as a positive force in society. As we move forward, embracing transparency will be key to unlocking AI's full potential while safeguarding the values we hold dear.

Now that we've explored the fundamentals of AI development, along with common applications and pitfalls, it's time to explore how AI is transforming industries, offering you new opportunities for innovation and growth.

Key Takeaways

- AI systems can inherit and perpetuate human biases, especially when trained on unbalanced or non-representative data—leading to unfair outcomes in hiring, healthcare, criminal justice, and more.

- Privacy is a growing concern as AI collects and analyzes vast amounts of personal data—often passively and without full user awareness—highlighting the need for stronger safeguards and informed consent.

- Laws like GDPR and CCPA aim to give individuals control over their data, enforcing transparency and ethical data use in AI systems.

- The "black box" problem makes it difficult to understand how many AI models make decisions, which can erode trust and accountability.

- Explainable AI (XAI) is an emerging solution to increase transparency by offering understandable explanations for AI decisions, helping users make informed choices and hold systems accountable.

- Ethical AI development requires proactive oversight, diverse participation, and regulatory compliance to ensure fairness, equity, and trustworthiness in AI applications.

Part 2
—
Hands-On with AI

Chapter 5

—

Getting Started with Text-Based AI

S tep into a conversation where every language is spoken—and instantly understood. Sounds like something out of a futuristic science fiction show, but it's a reality today.

That's the power of large language models (LLMs), which allow machines to process and generate human language with remarkable nuance. Tools like ChatGPT, Claude, Gemini, and Mistral are revolutionizing how we write, research, and communicate.

AI for Text Generation

LLMs are trained on large amounts of text data, using a method called self-supervised learning. This approach enables the model to learn patterns, structures, and nuances in language by predicting the next word in a sentence, given the previous words. As the model processes countless examples, it adjusts its parameters, refining its ability to generate coherent and contextually appropriate responses.

The sheer scale of these models is impressive, with parameters numbering in the billions, enabling them to understand and produce language in a way that mimics human conversation. This training process, though resource-intensive, equips LLMs with a deep understanding of language, empowering them to tackle complex tasks like summarization, translation, and even creative writing.

Each LLM has its unique strengths and weaknesses. ChatGPT, developed by OpenAI, is renowned for its conversational abilities, making it a great tool for chatbots and interactive applications. It excels at generating text that feels natural and engaging, though it sometimes struggles with factual accuracy.

Claude, by Anthropic, also shines in conversational contexts, with a focus on ethical considerations in AI interactions. It prioritizes alignment with human intentions, ensuring responses are safe and respectful.

Gemini, by Google, is designed for versatility, performing well across various tasks, from language generation to coding assistance. Its strength lies in adaptability, though it occasionally sacrifices depth for breadth.

Finally, Mistral, known for its efficiency and speed, is optimized for real-time applications, excelling in environments where quick responses are crucial, despite sometimes lacking the nuanced understanding of more comprehensive models.

The limitations of these LLMs often depend on whether you use a free or paid version. Free versions of models like ChatGPT offer significant functionality but may be limited in processing power, resulting in slower responses or restricted access to advanced features. These constraints can affect the model's ability to handle large datasets or complex queries, making them less suitable for demanding applications.

Paid subscriptions, on the other hand, unlock enhanced capabilities, such as faster response times and access to cutting-edge features, like real-time internet browsing or advanced analytics. This additional power comes at a cost, but it allows users to fully leverage the model's potential, offering a more robust and versatile tool for both personal and professional use.

Getting Started with ChatGPT: A Step-by-Step Guide

To get started with ChatGPT, you'll first need to access the website. Open your preferred web browser and type `chatgpt.com` into the search bar. When the site loads, you'll notice an option to either sign up or log in.

Note that you can use ChatGPT without creating an account. However, conversations will not be stored between sessions. If you want to keep a conversation going even after you've left and reloaded the web site, setting up an account is required.

If you already have an account, click the Log in button and follow the on-screen instructions. For new users, click on the Sign up for free button and follow the on-screen prompts. (Note: Companies frequently change their log-in and sign-up processes, so your exact steps may be different. Just follow the on-screen instructions, and you'll be fine.)

1. Enter your email address and click **Continue**.

2. Choose and enter a secure password (a minimum of 12 characters is required, and it is recommended to include a combination of upper case letters, lower case letters, numerals, and special characters such as ! @ # $, etc.), then click **Continue**.

3. You will receive an email with a six-digit verification code. Once you receive it, copy this code into the input box and click **Continue**.

4. You will then be prompted to enter your full name and birthday. Before doing so, you may want to review OpenAI's Terms and Privacy Policy. If you agree with these, enter the requested information, then click **Continue**.

5. Next, you'll be presented with a splash screen offering some tips for getting started. Review these, then when you're ready, click **Okay, let's go**.

6. Finally, you'll sign another announcement about ChatGPT's memory feature. This is your choice, but I recommend enabling this for deeper conversations and recall of past discussions. Click **Not now** or **Enable**.

You're now all set to investigate the capabilities of ChatGPT, a powerful tool for generating text based on your prompts.

As you embark on your first interactions with ChatGPT, having a set of prompts at your disposal can be incredibly helpful. These prompts serve as a gateway to discovering the model's versatility. Try starting with simple inquiries like **What's the weather like today?** or **Tell me a fun fact about space**. These openers can help you get a feel for how ChatGPT processes information and responds.

If you're curious about more specific topics, consider prompts like **Explain photosynthesis in simple terms** or **What are some tips for organizing a small apartment?**

For those interested in creative writing, prompts such as **Write a short poem about the sea** or **Generate a story set in a futuristic city** can be fun ways to experiment with narrative generation.

You might also explore practical prompts like **What are some healthy dinner ideas?** or **How can I improve my sleep habits?** Each query helps you understand different facets of ChatGPT's abilities.

When using ChatGPT, you might occasionally find its responses need clarification or rephrasing. To refine an answer, try using prompts like **Can you explain that differently?** or **What do you mean by that?** These requests encourage ChatGPT to present information in varied formats, enhancing your understanding.

If a response feels too complex, consider asking, **Can you simplify that explanation?** This approach helps tailor the conversation to your preferred level of detail and clarity.

Additionally, if a response seems off-topic, you can redirect the conversation with prompts such as **That's interesting, but can we focus on [specific topic]?** or **Let's revisit the main point.** This flexibility allows you to guide the dialogue, ensuring you extract the most relevant information.

Keeping a conversation with ChatGPT lively and engaging can be both fun and enriching. One way to sustain momentum is by building on previous exchanges. If you receive an intriguing answer, follow up with related questions like **How does that relate to [another topic]?** or **What are the implications of that?** This approach not only deepens the dialogue but also uncovers connections between topics.

You can also introduce hypothetical scenarios to explore creative possibilities, asking, **What if we applied this concept to [a new context]?** or **Imagine if [an event] happened--how would that affect [something else]?** These speculative questions invite creativity and broaden the conversation's scope.

For a more personalized experience, consider training ChatGPT to match your personal preferences and communication style. Start by consistently using language and tone that reflect your personality. Over time, ChatGPT will adapt to these nuances, tailoring its responses to better match your style. You can also provide feedback on its replies, indicating what you liked or found helpful, such as saying, **I appreciate the detailed explanation or I prefer shorter responses**.

This input helps ChatGPT fine-tune its interactions, creating a more customized and satisfying experience. Furthermore, using custom instructions or providing context about your preferences at the beginning of a session can guide ChatGPT in maintaining consistency throughout the conversation.

Using ChatGPT for Everyday Tasks

Imagine kicking off your day with a simple to-do list that includes writing emails, preparing blog content, and organizing meals for the week. Each task requires attention and creativity, but also demands time you may not have. Enter ChatGPT, a digital companion ready to assist with these daily challenges, offering support in ways that streamline your routine and free up your time for other pursuits.

When it comes to drafting emails, ChatGPT can be a lifesaver. Whether you need to compose a professional message or a friendly note, it provides suggestions and structures to help articulate your thoughts. Simply input your key points, and ChatGPT will generate a polished draft, ensuring you communicate effectively and efficiently. This capability allows you to focus on the content rather than getting bogged down by the nuances of tone or style.

For those involved in writing essays or blog posts, ChatGPT acts as both a muse and a collaborator. It helps brainstorm ideas, develop outlines, and even craft full paragraphs that flow seamlessly. If you're stuck on a particular section, ChatGPT can suggest ways to bridge gaps or provide alternative viewpoints.

This interaction doesn't replace your unique voice but enhances it, offering a fresh perspective or sparking inspiration when creativity stalls. By collaborating with ChatGPT, you can explore new angles and enrich your writing with depth and variety, making the process less daunting and more enjoyable.

Beyond writing, ChatGPT excels in the realm of research, gathering and organizing information swiftly. Whether you're exploring a new topic or seeking detailed data, ChatGPT can help summarize complex information into digestible bites. This feature is invaluable when you need to get up to speed on a subject quickly. Provide ChatGPT with a topic or question, and it will sift through vast amounts of information, presenting you with a clear, concise summary. This ability to distill information saves you hours of sifting through articles and reports, allowing you to focus on analysis and application instead.

In the kitchen, ChatGPT transforms meal planning and grocery shopping into a breeze. It can recommend meal plans based on dietary preferences or available ingredients, offering creative ways to use what you have on hand. If you're planning meals for the week, ChatGPT can generate a balanced menu, complete with shopping lists that ensure you have everything you need. This planning reduces the stress of mealtime decisions and helps maintain a healthy and varied diet. If you have specific dietary needs or goals, ChatGPT can tailor suggestions to align with nutritional guidelines, ensuring meals are both satisfying and health-conscious.

Consider asking ChatGPT to help plan a week's worth of dinners. It might suggest a mix of cuisines, from Italian pasta dishes to Asian stir-fries, providing recipes that introduce new flavors and techniques. It can also accommodate requests for quick meals on busy nights or elaborate dishes for leisurely weekends. Each suggestion comes with a list of ingredients, streamlining your shopping experience and minimizing waste. By taking the guesswork out of meal planning, ChatGPT allows you to enjoy the process of cooking and sharing meals without the burden of tedious preparation.

Grocery shopping becomes more efficient with ChatGPT's organizational prowess. It can categorize items by store section, ensuring a smooth flow as you navigate the aisles. This organization helps avoid forgotten items, reducing the need for last-minute trips.

Additionally, ChatGPT can suggest alternatives for unavailable ingredients or highlight sales and promotions, maximizing your budget and enhancing the shopping experience. This tool not only saves time but also turns a chore into an opportunity for discovery and creativity.

Using ChatGPT for Career Growth (or Change)

Picture yourself standing at a crossroads in your career, contemplating the next steps to take. You may have aspirations for growth in your current field, or perhaps you're considering a pivot to an entirely new industry. This is where ChatGPT can become an invaluable ally, offering guidance and resources to help you navigate these significant decisions.

Developing a career growth plan with ChatGPT involves a comprehensive evaluation of your current position and future aspirations. By engaging in interactive dialogue, you can outline specific career goals and identify the skills needed to achieve them. ChatGPT assists by suggesting potential pathways and resources, such as online courses, networking events, or industry certifications that align with your career objectives.

This personalized advice helps you create a roadmap for advancement, breaking down long-term goals into achievable milestones. With ChatGPT's support, you can gain clarity and direction, empowering you to take proactive steps toward your desired future.

If you're considering launching a side hustle, ChatGPT can help you explore viable opportunities and develop a strategic plan. It offers unique insights into market trends, which can help you identify niches where your skills and passions intersect. By analyzing data and offering creative suggestions, ChatGPT assists you in brainstorming potential business ideas that align with your interests and expertise.

Once you've settled on a concept, ChatGPT can lead you through the initial stages of setting up a side hustle. It can offer advice on creating a business plan, marketing strategies, and even ways to balance your time effectively between your primary job and new venture. This practical support ensures that your side hustle, in addition to generating income, brings personal fulfillment and growth.

In the realm of career change, ChatGPT acts as a mentor, helping you transition smoothly into a new field. It begins by assessing your transferable skills, identifying how your current experience can be leveraged in your new industry. This analysis is crucial, as it highlights the strengths you bring to the table and the areas where further development is needed. ChatGPT can then recommend specific skills improvement plans tailored to your target career.

It suggests relevant resources, such as e-learning platforms, workshops, or mentorship programs, that can accelerate your learning and adaptation. By providing actionable steps and keeping you motivated, ChatGPT supports your journey as you acquire the competencies necessary for your new role.

Furthermore, ChatGPT can assist in enhancing your professional presence, an essential aspect of career growth and change. Whether you're updating your resume or refining your LinkedIn profile, ChatGPT offers guidance on how best to present your skills and achievements.

It can help craft compelling narratives that resonate with potential employers or clients, ensuring your professional brand stands out. This personalized advice is particularly valuable in today's competitive job market, where a well-crafted digital presence can open doors to new opportunities. ChatGPT's insights help you communicate your value effectively, increasing your visibility and appeal to prospective employers or business partners.

Through each of these avenues, ChatGPT empowers you to take control of your career trajectory. It provides the tools and resources needed to make informed decisions, facilitate growth, and embrace change with confidence. By leveraging ChatGPT's capabilities, you can explore new career possibilities, develop a clear path forward, and take hold of the opportunities that align with your goals and aspirations.

As you continue to engage with ChatGPT, you'll find it not only supports your career ambitions but also enriches your personal development, encouraging lifelong learning and adaptability. With ChatGPT as your guide, the potential for career growth and transformation is boundless, limited only by your imagination and determination.

In navigating career growth or change, using ChatGPT allows for strategic planning and informed decision-making. The next step is to explore how AI can be integrated into creative processes and personal productivity, enhancing not only your career but also your daily life.

Key Takeaways

- Large Language Models (LLMs) like ChatGPT, Claude, Gemini, and Mistral are advanced AI systems trained on massive datasets to understand and generate human-like language. Each model has different strengths and priorities, from ChatGPT's conversational tone to Gemini's versatility, Claude's ethical focus, and Mistral's speed and efficiency.

- Using ChatGPT starts with basic prompts that guide the model's output—users can explore questions, creative writing, or practical tasks like summarizing or organizing ideas. Refining responses with follow-up prompts allows users to guide tone, depth, and topic relevance—turning ChatGPT into a flexible conversation partner.

- ChatGPT enhances everyday productivity, from writing emails and blog posts to meal planning and creating shopping lists—all through natural language interaction. It also supports career development, offering help with resume writing, skill-building, side-hustle planning, and identifying opportunities for growth or transition.

Sample Prompts

The possibilities for your exploration with ChatGPT (or any other text-based AI) are limited only by your imagination. As we've seen above, it's easy to get started. If you need some more ideas, though, here are some prompts in different areas to get the wheels turning.

Adapting to Retirement

- What are some meaningful hobbies or activities to explore in retirement?
- Help me create a weekly schedule that balances rest, fun, and personal growth.
- What are some ways to stay socially connected after leaving the workplace?
- Suggest volunteer opportunities that align with my interests and skills.
- Give me ideas for starting a part-time business or passion project in retirement.
- How can I maintain a sense of identity and purpose after retiring?
- Help me plan a realistic retirement travel budget and itinerary.
- What are some daily routines that support physical and mental wellness after 60?
- Can you recommend online courses or workshops for lifelong learning in retirement?
- What are some tips for downsizing my home while preserving memories?

Cooking

- Suggest easy weeknight dinner recipes.
- How do I make homemade pasta from scratch?

- What are some vegan substitutes for eggs?
- Give me a step-by-step guide to baking sourdough bread.
- Can you generate a grocery list for a Mediterranean diet?
- Create a 5-day meal plan for a family of four.
- How can I batch cook for the week ahead?
- What are common spices used in Indian cuisine?
- Suggest creative uses for leftover roast chicken.
- What's the best way to grill vegetables evenly?

Creative Writing

- Write the opening paragraph of a mystery novel set in a lighthouse during a storm.
- Create a compelling backstory for a villain who used to be a hero.
- Generate 10 fantasy character names with a short description for each.
- Help me outline a short story about time travel and unintended consequences.
- What are some creative writing exercises to overcome writer's block?
- Rewrite this sentence in a more poetic or lyrical style: 'She walked into the room quietly.'
- Describe a futuristic city where nature and technology have merged.
- Give me 5 plot twists I could use in a romantic comedy.
- Write a dialogue between two characters who are meeting again after 20 years apart.
- Help me brainstorm a title and tagline for a dystopian young adult novel.

Education & Learning

- Can you explain the concept of photosynthesis in simple terms for a 7th grader?
- Create a study schedule to help me prepare for a final exam in two weeks.
- What are the best memorization techniques for learning vocabulary?
- Summarize the main ideas from Plato's Republic in a few paragraphs.
- Help me understand how to solve a quadratic equation step-by-step.
- Suggest fun ways to teach fractions to elementary school students.
- What are the key differences between the American and British education systems?
- Generate quiz questions to help me practice for a U.S. history test.
- How can I stay focused while studying with ADHD?
- Recommend free online resources for learning data science as a beginner.

Entertainment

- Give me a list of must-watch sci-fi movies from the past 10 years.
- What are some underrated comedy shows on streaming platforms right now?
- Can you recommend a feel-good movie for a cozy weekend?"
- Create a themed movie night plan, including snacks and a double feature.
- Suggest some family-friendly board games for game night.
- Who are the top 5 breakout music artists this year across different genres?

- Summarize the plot of 'Stranger Things' without spoilers.
- What's the difference between Marvel and DC superheroes?
- Help me plan a trivia night with questions from popular TV shows.
- Recommend some binge-worthy podcasts for true crime fans.

Event Planning

- Help me plan a backyard birthday party for 20 guests on a $300 budget.
- What's a simple timeline for organizing a wedding one year in advance?
- Suggest creative themes and activities for a kids' Halloween party.
- Generate a checklist for hosting a professional networking event.
- What are some fun, low-cost team-building ideas for a company retreat?
- Can you help me write an invitation message for a casual dinner party?
- What's the best way to coordinate RSVPs and dietary restrictions digitally?
- Give me tips for planning a stress-free holiday gathering for family and friends.
- How can I decorate a small venue for a baby shower without spending too much?
- Create a week-of checklist for a graduation party with 50+ guests.

Gardening & Lawncare

- What are the best vegetables to plant in early spring in my region?

- Help me plan a low-maintenance flower garden that attracts pollinators.

- How do I start a compost pile, and what can I safely include?

- Create a monthly lawn care checklist for my climate zone.

- What are some natural ways to get rid of aphids on tomato plants?

- Suggest companion planting combinations for a small backyard garden.

- How do I revive a patchy, brown lawn without reseeding the whole yard?

- Generate a beginner's guide to indoor herb gardening.

- What tools do I really need to start gardening on a budget?

- Can you help me design a balcony container garden with herbs and flowers?

Health & Wellness

- Suggest a beginner-friendly morning routine that boosts energy and focus.

- What are some healthy snack ideas that are high in protein?

- Can you explain the difference between mindfulness and meditation?

- Create a 7-day wellness challenge to help me improve my habits.

- What are effective ways to reduce stress naturally during a busy workday?

- Give me a list of gentle stretches I can do at my desk.

- Help me track my water intake with a simple daily checklist.

- What are the benefits of walking 30 minutes a day?

- Can you generate a balanced meal plan for someone trying to eat clean?

- What are signs of burnout, and how can I recover from it?

Home Improvement

- What are the best ways to soundproof a room?
- How do I install a smart thermostat?
- Tips for renovating a small bathroom on a budget.
- What tools do I need to build a deck?
- Can you help design a garage storage system?
- How do I repair a cracked drywall corner?
- Create a maintenance checklist for my home.
- What's the easiest way to paint kitchen cabinets?
- Help me choose between vinyl and wood flooring.
- Generate a plan to upgrade my home's curb appeal.

Interior Design

- Help me choose a color palette for a small living room that feels cozy and bright.
- What's the difference between modern, contemporary, and minimalist interior styles?
- Suggest affordable ways to refresh my bedroom without major renovations.
- How can I make a studio apartment feel more spacious and functional?
- Create a mood board idea for a nature-inspired home office.
- What are some stylish storage solutions for small spaces?
- Generate a checklist for redecorating a guest bathroom on a budget.
- How do I mix and match furniture styles without it looking chaotic?

- What are the best indoor plants for low-light rooms, and how do I style them?
- Design a layout for a shared kids' bedroom that's both fun and organized.

Job Hunting

- Help me write a professional resume for a customer service position.
- Can you suggest strong bullet points for my experience as a retail manager?
- What are some common interview questions for entry-level tech roles, and how should I answer them?
- Draft a personalized cover letter for a marketing job at a startup.
- What skills are most in-demand for remote jobs right now?
- Help me improve my LinkedIn summary to attract recruiters.
- How do I explain a gap in employment on my resume or in an interview?
- Suggest job search websites and tools for creative professionals.
- Can you generate a list of questions I should ask at the end of a job interview?
- Give me a step-by-step plan to switch from teaching to a corporate training career.

Parenting

- What are some fun and educational activities for a 4-year-old on a rainy day?
- Help me create a bedtime routine for a toddler who resists going to sleep.
- What's the best way to talk to my child about managing big emotions?

- Can you suggest age-appropriate chores for kids between 5 and 10 years old?

- Generate lunchbox meal ideas that are healthy and picky-eater approved.

- What are some tips for setting screen time boundaries for different age groups?

- How can I support my child during their transition to a new school?

- Give me talking points for discussing bullying with my child in a supportive way.

- Suggest a weekly family schedule that balances school, chores, and quality time.

- What are the best ways to encourage reading habits in early elementary children?

Personal Finance

- Can you help me create a simple monthly budget based on my income and expenses?

- Explain the difference between a traditional IRA and a Roth IRA in simple terms.

- Give me 5 strategies to save money on groceries without using coupons.

- What's the 50/30/20 budgeting rule, and how do I apply it to my finances?

- Help me come up with a debt repayment plan using the snowball method.

- What are some beginner-friendly ways to start investing with $100?

- Can you generate a financial checklist for someone in their 30s?

- How do credit scores work, and what can I do to improve mine?

- Compare the pros and cons of buying vs. leasing a car.

- Suggest apps or tools that can help me track spending and savings goals.

Pet Care

- What's a good daily care routine for a first-time dog owner?
- How can I safely introduce a new cat to a home with an older dog?
- Suggest enrichment activities for a high-energy indoor cat.
- What human foods are safe (and unsafe) for dogs to eat?
- Help me create a checklist for adopting a rescue pet.
- What are early signs of illness in rabbits or other small pets?
- Can you recommend a weekly grooming routine for a long-haired dog?
- What's the best way to crate train a puppy without causing stress?
- Give me tips for keeping a pet bird healthy and mentally stimulated.
- How can I help my pet adjust to being home alone during the workday?

Self-Help & Motivation

- Give me a motivational quote and a short reflection to start my day with intention.
- Help me create a 30-day self-improvement challenge focused on mindset and habits.
- What are 5 strategies I can use to stay motivated when I feel overwhelmed?
- Can you suggest a simple morning routine to boost mental clarity and energy?
- Write a short pep talk for someone doubting their ability to succeed.
- What are the signs of self-sabotage, and how can I overcome them?
- Generate journal prompts to help me explore my goals and values.

- Suggest affirmations to help build self-confidence and resilience.
- Give me a weekly reflection worksheet for tracking my emotional and mental well-being.
- How can I break a bad habit and replace it with something positive?

Small Business

- Help me brainstorm a name and tagline for a handmade soap business.
- What are the first legal steps I need to take to start a small business?
- Generate a simple business plan outline for a freelance graphic designer.
- How can I attract more local customers to my coffee shop?
- What are cost-effective marketing strategies for a new online store?
- Suggest tools to help manage inventory, orders, and shipping for my small business.
- Can you draft a professional email template to pitch my services to new clients?
- What social media platforms should I focus on for a fitness coaching business?
- Create a content calendar with weekly post ideas for my small business blog.
- Explain the difference between an LLC and a sole proprietorship in simple terms.

Sustainable Living

- What are 5 simple changes I can make at home to reduce my environmental impact?
- Help me create a weekly meal plan that minimizes food waste and packaging.

- Suggest beginner-friendly ways to start composting in an apartment.

- What are some eco-friendly alternatives to single-use plastic in the kitchen?

- Generate a list of sustainable gift ideas for birthdays or holidays.

- How can I reduce energy consumption in my home without major renovations?

- Explain the difference between biodegradable, compostable, and recyclable products.

- What should I look for when shopping for ethically made clothing?

- Give me tips for creating a zero-waste travel kit.

- Help me organize a neighborhood cleanup or sustainability-themed event.

Technology & Gadgets

- What are the must-have tech gadgets for a home office setup?

- Explain the difference between SSD and HDD in simple terms.

- Can you help me choose a budget-friendly laptop for everyday use?

- What are the pros and cons of switching to a smart home system?

- Compare the latest smartphones from Apple, Samsung, and Google.

- Suggest beginner-friendly tools for home automation (lights, plugs, etc.).

- How do I back up my data securely using cloud storage?

- Generate a checklist for setting up a new WiFi router at home.

- What are some useful mobile apps for managing daily life or boosting productivity?

- Explain how Bluetooth works and how to fix common pairing issues.

Time Management

- How do I prioritize my daily tasks?
- Suggest a morning routine for better productivity.
- Tips for managing time as a remote worker.
- How can I limit distractions while working from home?
- Create a weekly schedule template with time blocks.
- How do I beat procrastination effectively?
- What are the best time tracking apps?
- Give me a plan for organizing my digital files.
- Help me create a time audit worksheet.
- Generate a checklist to prepare for Monday mornings.

Travel Planning

- Help me plan a 7-day trip to Italy, including top sights and local food recommendations.
- What are the essential items I should pack for an international vacation?
- Can you suggest family-friendly travel destinations within the U.S.?
- Create a weekend getaway itinerary within 3 hours of my city.
- How can I find the best deals on flights and hotels?
- What cultural etiquette tips should I know before visiting Japan?
- Generate a travel checklist for a first-time traveler.
- What are some solo travel safety tips for women?
- Recommend scenic train routes in Europe for a relaxed travel experience.
- Can you help me organize my trip using Google Maps or a travel planning app?

Workplace Efficiency

- You are an expert data analyst. Review the following spreadsheet data and summarize the key trends, outliers, and potential concerns. Focus on identifying any patterns or actionable insights.

- You are preparing a report for executives. Based on the spreadsheet data I provide, generate a 3-paragraph executive summary highlighting major metrics, wins, and any risks.

- Assume you are a business consultant. After reviewing the provided spreadsheet (containing sales/expenses/ performance metrics), recommend three ways the business could improve operations or increase revenue.

- Act as a quality control auditor. Check this spreadsheet for obvious errors, inconsistencies, or missing data points, and suggest corrections."

- You are a professional editor specializing in business communications. Review the following draft report for clarity, grammar, and professionalism. Suggest improvements in wording where appropriate.

- You are creating an executive briefing. Summarize the following report into no more than 10 concise bullet points, focusing only on the most critical information.

- Review the following draft email/report and suggest adjustments to make it more professional, courteous, and appropriate for a corporate audience.

- You are a project manager. Based on the following meeting notes or report, extract a list of actionable next steps, who is responsible for each, and a suggested deadline.

- You are a business process consultant. Based on the following description of my daily tasks [insert tasks], suggest 5 specific processes that could be automated to save time and increase accuracy.

- You are an expert productivity coach. Based on this list of tasks [insert list], prioritize them in order of highest business impact, and suggest which tasks could be delegated or automated.

- You are a management consultant. Based on the following spreadsheet data, create an outline for a 5-slide

PowerPoint presentation summarizing key findings, actionable recommendations, and next steps. Provide suggested slide titles and bullet points for each slide. (Variation: You could also ask for full speaker notes.)

- You are a professional proposal writer. Using the following project details [insert scope, objectives, deadlines, budget], draft a client proposal that is persuasive, clearly structured, and highlights the company's strengths. (You can even specify: 'Format it in standard proposal sections: Executive Summary, Project Scope, Deliverables, Timeline, Pricing, and Closing.')

- Act as a strategic consultant. Based on the following project options [insert options], create a decision matrix evaluating them by criteria such as cost, time to completion, ROI, and strategic fit. Recommend the best choice with a short justification. (Stretch Goal: Ask AI to output it as a simple table too!)

- You are a senior executive assistant. Based on the following meeting notes or project summary, draft a concise and professional email to update a stakeholder on the current status, key achievements, and immediate next steps. Keep the tone positive, informative, and action-focused.

- Imagine you are designing a client onboarding checklist. Based on the following business type and services [insert info], create a detailed checklist of all steps, documents, and actions needed to successfully onboard a new client.

Make a Difference with Your Review
—
Unlock the Power of Generosity

The best way to find yourself is to lose yourself in the service of others.

—Mahatma Gandhi

When you give without expecting anything back, something powerful happens. You feel good. You help others. You make the world just a little better. So let's do that—together.

Are you someone who once felt unsure about AI, not sure where to begin? Then you know how it feels to take that first step. My mission with this book is simple: To help people understand AI in a clear, easy way—so they can use it to grow, thrive, and keep up in a changing world.

But I can't do it alone.

Most people decide whether or not to try a book based on what other readers say. That's where you come in.

Would you take one minute to help someone just like you?

Your review—just a few honest words—can open the door for someone who's still unsure. It might be the nudge they need to:

- Start a business that helps their family or community
- Land a better job that brings more meaning to their life
- Learn new skills and take control of their future
- Feel less overwhelmed and more confident about technology
- Or even just take that first step into something new

It costs nothing. But it means everything.

To leave a review, just scan the QR code or follow this link: `https://www.amazon.com/review/review-your-purchases/?asin=1732755183`

If you enjoy helping others grow, you're my kind of person. Thank you—truly—for being part of this journey.

—Morgan Hale

Chapter 6

—

Creating Images from Text

A painter stands in front of a blank canvas, with a spectrum of colors at their fingertips but no brush in hand. Now, picture a technology that transforms this scene, allowing the artist to conjure vivid imagery by merely speaking or typing words.

This is the realm of Text-to-Image (TTI) generation models, where written prompts give life to visual art. These models, including DALL·E, Midjourney, and Ideogram, and Stable Diffusion, represent a frontier where language and imagery converge, offering you the power to create stunning visuals without traditional artistic tools.

Getting Started with Text-to-Image

DALL·E (a play on the names of surrealist artist Salvador Dalí and the Disney-Pixar animated robot WALL·E) stands out for its user-friendly interface and rapid generation of high-quality images. It's designed to interpret and execute prompts with remarkable precision, making it a go-to for those seeking detailed and visually appealing results quickly.

Based on a diffusion model, DALL·E uses a sophisticated technique that gradually refines an image from random noise to a coherent picture. This process mimics natural diffusion, ensuring each image generated is both unique and contextually rich. The model's ability to understand nuanced prompts makes it particularly useful for complex projects like logo design and marketing visuals.

Midjourney takes a different approach, emphasizing aesthetics and artistic flair. Accessible via the community app Discord, it caters to users who prioritize creativity and visual impact over technical detail. Unlike DALL·E, which excels in fidelity, Midjourney focuses on style and emotion, often producing images that feel more like art than digital renderings. This distinction makes it ideal for projects where mood and tone are paramount, such as conceptual art and storytelling. Midjourney's emphasis on visual storytelling allows you to explore new artistic directions, leveraging AI to push the boundaries of creative expression.

Ideogram, though less prominent, offers a unique feature set tailored for educational and design applications. It excels in creating diagrams and infographics, providing structured visuals that communicate complex information clearly. This model is particularly beneficial for educators and content creators who need to convey data and concepts visually. By transforming text into organized graphics, Ideogram streamlines the process of creating educational materials, enhancing learning and engagement.

Stable Diffusion, an open-source model, champions accessibility and flexibility. It uses the Latent Diffusion Model, which operates efficiently on consumer-grade hardware, making it a viable option for hobbyists and professionals alike. As an open-source tool, Stable Diffusion fosters a collaborative community where users contribute to its development and share enhancements. This model's open nature encourages experimentation and innovation, offering a platform for those interested in customizing and extending AI capabilities. Its adaptability and community-driven ethos make it a favorite among tech enthusiasts and developers.

Despite their strengths, these TTI models also have limitations. DALL·E's user-friendly nature might not suit those seeking extensive customization or control over image generation. Midjourney, while visually striking, can sometimes prioritize style over detail, leading to less realistic outputs. Ideogram's focus on structured visuals limits its application for freeform artistic endeavors. Stable Diffusion's open-source framework, while advantageous for customization, requires a fair amount of technical expertise to fully utilize.

The availability of these models often comes in two tiers: free and paid. Free versions provide a glimpse into their capabilities but typically impose restrictions on usage volume, resolution, or advanced features. For instance, DALL·E's free version might limit the number of images you can generate per day or the resolution available. In contrast, paid subscriptions unlock enhanced capabilities, such as higher output quality, faster processing times, and access to additional features like real-time collaboration or expanded datasets. These premium options are particularly appealing for professionals who rely on AI-generated imagery for commercial purposes, where quality and efficiency are critical.

A Step-by-Step Guide to DALL·E

To begin creating images with DALL·E, you'll first need access to ChatGPT, as outlined in the previous chapter. Once your ChatGPT account is set up, accessing DALL·E becomes a seamless process. You'll find DALL·E integrated into the ChatGPT interface, with even more functionality if you have a Plus subscription. This integration enables you to switch easily between generating text and images, enhancing your creative capabilities.

Simply log into your ChatGPT account and navigate to the DALL·E interface. To do this, click the extended menu (**...**) button in the prompt box and select **Create image**. Alternately, simply type **Show me** into the regular prompt bar, followed by what you want to see. ChatGPT will recognize that you're asking for an image and relay the prompt to the DALL·E engine. This easy accessibility not only simplifies the process but also makes it an enjoyable experience, letting you focus on your creativity rather than the technical aspects of the tool.

As you embark on your first ventures with DALL·E, starting with straightforward prompts is beneficial. For beginners, consider using prompts that are clear and descriptive to see how effectively DALL·E captures your vision.

(Note: The color images of the following prompts can also be found on the resources page at adbooks.pub/resources.)

Try a prompt like **a sunset over a bridge spanning a wide river**. This prompt combines elements of both nature and technology, along with color and composition. It allows DALL·E to showcase its ability to capture complex scenes.

a sunset over a bridge spanning a wide river

By default, DALL·E will typically generate square images. If you prefer landscape (wide) or portrait (tall) views, add that to your prompt. You can even get more precise by specifying your desired aspect ratio, such as 4:3, 3:5, or 2:3, where the first number indicates the relative width and the second indicates the relative height of the image. A square image, of course, would have an aspect ratio of 1:1.

Another engaging prompt could be **a futuristic city skyline at night**, which challenges DALL·E to blend architectural elements with atmospheric lighting.

These prompts serve as an entry point, helping you understand how different elements influence the generated image. They also highlight DALL·E's strengths in rendering detailed and dynamic visuals, reflecting the richness of your imagination.

Once you've generated an image, refining it is where the magic really unfolds. DALL·E allows you to modify your prompts to adjust or enhance the image, making it more aligned with your vision. Suppose the initial image lacks the vibrancy you envisioned in the sunset. You can refine it by adding specific color details or lighting conditions, like **add a golden hue to the sunset** or **increase the brightness of the river reflection**.

This iterative process of refinement lets you explore various aspects of the image, adjusting elements until the result matches your expectations. These modifications enhance the creative process, offering you the ability to experiment with different visual styles and elements.

a futuristic city skyline at night

To explore DALL·E's capabilities further, try experimenting with prompts that introduce unusual combinations or imaginative scenes. For example, **an elephant playing a piano in a rainforest** challenges DALL·E to merge disparate elements into a coherent image.

This kind of prompt not only tests the model's versatility but also sparks creativity by pushing the boundaries of conventional imagery. As you refine such images, consider the details that define the scene—like the texture of the elephant's skin or the lushness of the rainforest. Modify the prompt to emphasize these details, achieving a more vivid and engaging visual result.

To maintain creative momentum, consider keeping a journal or digital document where you record your prompts and the resulting images. This practice helps track your creative journey, providing insights into how different prompts yield varied results. It also encourages reflection on which prompts work best and why, guiding future explorations.

Additionally, sharing your creations with a community, such as an online forum or social media group, can offer valuable feedback and inspiration. Engaging with others passionate about AI and creativity opens doors to new ideas and collaborations, enriching your experience with DALL·E.

an elephant playing a piano in a rainforest

Getting Creative with DALL·E

Imagine stepping into an art gallery where each piece is not just a painting but a fusion of styles, each one a testament to creativity without boundaries. With DALL·E, you have the opportunity to explore and create such masterpieces, discovering a myriad of art styles that can transform a simple idea into an extraordinary visual experience.

Whether you lean towards the bold strokes of Impressionism, the abstract forms of Cubism, or the intricate patterns of Art Nouveau, DALL·E is your canvas, ready to bring these styles to life with a simple prompt. Exploring different art styles allows you to see how the same concept can be interpreted in diverse ways, each with its own unique flair and emotion.

By experimenting with styles, you not only broaden your artistic horizon but also gain insights into how different elements—like color, texture, and composition—work together to create a harmonious piece.

Consider the elegance of Impressionism, where light and color play pivotal roles. You might prompt DALL·E with **a garden at dawn in the style of Impressionism**, resulting in a soft blend of pastels and gentle brushstrokes that capture the fleeting beauty of early morning light.

a garden at dawn in the style of Impressionism

The scene, alive with subtle hues and a sense of movement, evokes a tranquil yet vibrant atmosphere. In contrast, think about setting the same garden scene with a Cubist twist. A prompt like **a garden at dawn in Cubist style** could transform the serene landscape into an array of geometric shapes and fragmented perspectives, challenging the viewer's perception and inviting them to engage with the piece on a deeper level. The stark lines and angles introduce an element of abstraction, offering a fresh take on familiar scenery.

For those with a penchant for the whimsical, Art Nouveau offers a delightful playground. Using a prompt such as **a garden at dawn in Art Nouveau style**, DALL·E might render the scene with flowing lines and intricate details, reminiscent of the organic forms that define this style. The result could be an enchanting tapestry of nature, where every leaf and petal is meticulously crafted to create a sense of harmony and elegance.

a garden at dawn in Cubist style

This style's emphasis on decoration and linear patterns adds a layer of sophistication and charm, turning a simple garden into a work of art. These transformations showcase DALL·E's versatility and power to adapt a single concept across multiple artistic expressions.

Now, imagine combining these styles to create something truly unique. A prompt like **a garden at dawn blending Impressionism and Art Nouveau** could yield a scene where the gentle brushstrokes of Impressionism meet the ornate details of Art Nouveau.

a garden at dawn in Art Nouveau style

The garden would come alive with a dynamic interplay of light, color, and form, offering a rich visual experience that draws the viewer in. The fusion of styles not only highlights DALL·E's ability to merge different artistic elements but also inspires you to think beyond traditional boundaries, encouraging innovation and creativity. This approach allows you to experiment with hybrid styles, exploring how different artistic techniques complement and enhance each other.

a garden at dawn blending Impressionism and Art Nouveau

Consider the possibilities of blending Cubism with a touch of Surrealism. A prompt such as **a garden at dawn in a Cubist-Surrealist fusion** might produce an image where fragmented shapes coexist with dreamlike elements, creating a world that is both familiar and fantastical.

The juxtaposition of abstract geometry with surreal, unexpected details challenges conventional perceptions and invites viewers to explore new dimensions of reality. This creative process not only pushes the limits of what

a garden at dawn in a Cubist-Surrealist fusion

can be achieved with AI but also encourages you to embrace the unexpected, finding beauty in the unconventional.

As you experiment with DALL·E, remember that each creation is a reflection of your imagination and vision. The ability to transform a single idea through various styles and combinations offers endless opportunities for discovery and expression. Whether you're an artist who want to expand your repertoire or someone looking to explore new creative avenues, DALL·E provides the tools to visualize your ideas in ways that were once thought impossible.

Hands-On: Creating a Comic Strip with ChatGPT and DALL·E

If you were anything like me as a kid, you loved picking up the daily newspaper after the adults had finished and poring over the comic strips, especially on Sundays with the large, color format. There's a brilliance to this type of short-form storytelling, where each panel holds the power to advance the plot in a way that is both captivating and visually compelling—even if it's just a knock-knock joke.

Combining the word-smithing genius of ChatGPT with the artistic brilliance of DALL·E, you can now create your own four-panel comic strip, turning your ideas into art with just a few well-crafted prompts. The process begins with crafting a narrative that captures attention and maintains it through to the punchline.

In a four-panel strip, each image serves a particular function in the story. First is the Setup, which introduces your characters and sets the scene. This image generates reader interest and establishes the style and tone of the story you're weaving. Is this a gritty serial detective story, a day in the life of a wise-cracking iguana, or a slapstick pun-fest set among the ancient Aztecs? The job of the Setup is to convey this information.

With the stage set, the Conflict introduces the central theme or problem that is the focus of the strip. The text and image draw the readers in and spark their curiosity about how the story will develop. The Conflict should be clear and compelling, setting the wheels of the narrative in motion.

Next comes the Escalation, ramping up the tension and suspense. This is where you engage your readers and draw them further into the unfolding drama (or comedy or absurdity). The Escalation panel is crucial for maintaining momentum, ensuring that readers remain invested enough to get to the final panel.

At last, the Punchline delivers a satisfying resolution, often with a twist or a humorous conclusion. This panel is your chance to leave the readers with a sense of closure and a smile. The Punchline ties the narrative together, reinforcing the comic's theme and leaving a lasting impression.

To create a naturally flowing comic strip, each image must connect seamlessly with the next, maintaining consistency in style and character portrayal. DALL·E allows you to refine each panel, ensuring that the graphics align with your vision for the story. By adjusting prompts and tweaking details, you can achieve coherence across the entire strip, creating a unified narrative that captivates and entertains.

As you experiment with DALL·E, consider how each panel fits into the broader narrative. Think about the pacing and how the story unfolds visually. Are there opportunities to add layers to the plot or enrich the characters? By thoughtfully crafting each prompt and image, you can create a comic strip that not only tells a story but also resonates with readers on multiple levels.

Now that you have the basics, let's go step-by-step through the process of idea generation, script development, and finally crafting the images to suit the story or joke.

Hard Drive: A Jake Byte Mystery

A grizzled private eye in a digitized city, solving crimes in the shadows of the algorithmic age.

To begin your new side gig as a comic artist, you need a subject, style, and title. This is right in ChatGPT's wheelhouse.

```
Make up a title for a gritty serial detective comic
strip and give me a sample storyboard outline for a 4-
panel strip including Setup, Conflict, Escalation, and
Punchline/Resolution.
```

In addition to the title and description shown above, here's the rest of the output I received:

4-Panel Strip: "Echo Chamber" — Storyboard Outline

Panel 1—Setup

Caption: "It started with a whisper in a comment thread…"

Visual: Rain-slick alley at night, Jake Byte—trench coat, glowing cyber-eye—leans against a lamppost, scrolling a holoscreen projected from his wristwatch. He squints at a suspicious social media post.

Dialogue (Jake internal monologue): "Bot chatter's getting sloppy. Someone's hiding in plain sight."

Panel 2—Conflict

Visual: Jake steps into a shadowy basement office, confronting a nervous young coder (hoodie, dark circles, surrounded by glowing servers).

Coder: "It wasn't me! I just trained the model!"

Jake: "Then why's your neural net echoing hate like a war drum?"

Panel 3—Escalation

Visual: Close-up of a monitor showing a looping comment thread spiraling into chaos—AI-generated posts fueling outrage. Jake plugs in a sleek, glowing USB drive labeled "GPT-Sniffer."

Jake: "Let's see what your ghostwriter has to say…"

Panel 4—Punchline/Resolution

> Visual: Jake stands over a smoldering chatbot interface on-screen, its last words blinking, "I only amplified what you gave me."

> Caption: "In this city, even the truth needs a moderator."

> Jake (monologue): "Free speech is cheap. Intent costs extra."

Your output will be something different, of course, but my AI assistant has already been seasoned with my wry, funny-to-me sense of humor. Feel free to use the prompts to generate more options, refine the story elements, or tweak the visual descriptions. Once you're happy with the outline, start generating the images. Since DALL·E still has occasional challenges in producing reliable text, we'll ask ChatGPT to provide any dialog within the image caption.

```
Provide a 4-panel comic strip based on this storyboard.
Print related captions and dialog beneath the
respective panels.
```

Before you send this off to your local paper for syndication, you may need to touch it up in a graphic design tool like Adobe Photoshop, Affinity Photo, or Corel Paintshop. These are outside the scope of this book, but there are plenty of other great books and online resources to guide you in the process. For now, let's take a look at the other styles.

Iggy & Letty

A wise-cracking iguana (Iggy) and his long-suffering human roommate (Letty) navigate the chaos of everyday life—one sarcastic scale at a time.

Tlachtli Fools

A riotous romp through the Aztec empire, where ballplayers, priests, and warriors fumble their way through sacred rituals, political drama, and really bad puns.

Of course, nothing's perfect right out of the chute, but with a little refinement of the prompts, and some third-party editing software, AI can get you off to a great start.

Key Takeaways

- Text-to-Image (TTI) models like DALL·E, Midjourney, Ideogram, and Stable Diffusion allow users to generate detailed visual art using written prompts, bridging language and imagery.

- DALL·E is integrated into ChatGPT, allowing users to create and refine images through conversational interaction.

- Users can experiment with different artistic styles, such as Impressionism or Art Nouveau, and even blend them for hybrid visuals.

Chapter 7

—

AI-Powered Translation, Text-to-Speech & Text-to-Music

I magine reading your favorite novel in the original language—even if you don't speak it. Even better, not only do you understand every word, you don't even have to turn the pages. Your AI-powered digital narrator brings the story to life, in your native language, with clarity and expression.

While professionally produced audiobooks feature human voice actors and are typically released by publishers under specific licensing agreements, text-to-speech (TTS) technology offers a different experience: AI-generated narration of any written text, often on demand. When paired with AI-powered translation, an entire world of stories is now open to you.

TTS has transformed how we consume information, enhancing accessibility for those with visual impairments or reading difficulties, and offering a flexible alternative for those who prefer to listen. This chapter introduces you to TTS tools like NaturalReader, Speechify, and ElevenLabs, each with unique capabilities for converting text into lifelike audio—while also highlighting important considerations around usage rights and content ownership.

AI-Powered Language Translation

DeepL (deepl.com) is a leading translation tool known for its exceptional linguistic accuracy and nuanced understanding of context, setting it apart from traditional machine translators. Its intuitive interface and high-quality output have made it a favorite among writers, students, and professionals who require polished, human-like translations. DeepL supports multiple languages and offers tone adjustment options, making it ideal for both casual use and formal communication.

DeepL's technology is built on neural machine translation (NMT), utilizing deep learning and natural language processing (NLP) to interpret context, idiomatic expressions, and grammatical subtleties. Unlike earlier statistical translation models, NMT systems like DeepL aim to capture meaning rather than just replacing words, resulting in smoother, more natural translations.

Varying subscription levels, from free to professional, are available with DeepL. Limitations in the free version include capped document translations and limited customization options for tone and style. Paid plans unlock advanced features like unlimited text translations, expanded document translation support, application programming interface (API) access for developers, and enhanced data security. For professional writers, translators, and businesses, these subscriptions offer significant advantages, providing greater flexibility, speed, and privacy in translation workflows.

DeepL hasn't quite reached the level of *Star Trek*'s universal translator, but with its speech-to-text and text-to-speech options—with language translation in between—the future is closer than you might think. Unfortunately, translations for Klingon, Dothraki, and Elvish are not yet available.

While DeepL is incredibly powerful, it's not alone in the field. Google Translate (translate.google.com) is a versatile option for quick, general-purpose translations, offering broad language support and integration across devices. While effective for simple tasks, it may struggle with preserving nuance in more complex texts. Microsoft Translator (translator.microsoft.com) similarly caters to wide audiences, providing translation services for individuals and businesses, with emphasis on real-time conversation translation.

Each translation tool has its strengths and limitations. DeepL is widely praised for fluency and naturalness but may lag behind competitors in the total number of languages supported. Google Translate's advantage lies in its massive language library and integration, though accuracy can vary.

Microsoft Translator's strength is real-time conversation support, although its written translation quality sometimes feels mechanical compared to DeepL.

Getting Started with Text-to-Speech

NaturalReader is a user-friendly TTS tool known for its natural-sounding voices and optical character recognition (OCR) feature, which allows users to convert scanned documents into speech. It's especially popular among students and educators for its ability to bring written content to auditory life. NaturalReader offers a range of voices and accents, making it suitable for international audiences.

Speechify, initially developed to assist individuals with reading challenges, now serves a broader audience, offering versatile reading options with a focus on ease and accessibility. It excels in catering to users with specific reading needs, providing customizable playback speeds and highlighting text as it reads aloud.

ElevenLabs integrates advanced AI for high-quality, emotionally resonant audio, catering to creators and audio engineers seeking lifelike speech output. This model focuses on high-quality audio output, capturing subtle nuances in speech for a more immersive experience.

Training TTS models involves using AI and natural language processing (NLP) to analyze text and generate speech. These models learn from vast datasets, mimicking human speech patterns to produce clear and contextually accurate audio. Unlike large language models that focus on generating coherent text, TTS models prioritize transforming written words into speech, emphasizing pronunciation and intonation.

The strengths of TTS models lie in their ability to provide diverse voice options and language support. However, each model has its limitations. NaturalReader's free version may lack advanced features, while Speechify's premium plan can be costly for casual users. ElevenLabs, though offering superior audio quality, requires a subscription to gain full access to its capabilities.

The free versions of these TTS tools provide basic functionality, allowing users to explore core features without financial commitment. However, limitations may include restricted voice options, limited text conversion, and reduced audio quality.

Paid subscriptions unlock enhanced features, such as access to premium voices, unlimited text-to-speech conversion, and advanced audio editing tools. Subscriptions can be worthwhile for those who rely heavily on TTS for accessibility, content creation, or professional use, as they provide a more comprehensive and tailored experience.

A Step-by-Step Guide to NaturalReader

Getting started with NaturalReader is not complicated, but the area of choices can be a bit daunting. To begin, direct your browse to the NaturalReader website, naturalreaders.com. You'll have a number of options for language and voice models, but for now, just click on **Get Started for Free→**. Another tab will open, with more language and voice options. Just click on **Next**.

You will now have the option to select between personal use (text-to-speech) or commercial use (voice generation). Voice generation is where Natural Reader's power really shines, but to get started, choose **Go to A.I. Text to Speech**.

Now, you can explore the range of available options. First, browse through the selection of prepared voice options by clicking on the portrait in the upper control bar. To level-set your expectations, click on the **Free** tab and explore the available options by mousing over each of the voice panels and clicking the speaker icon. If you've used the Accessibility features built in to Microsoft Windows, you'll recognize these voices. While they're better than the robotic voices of a few years ago, it's unlikely you would ever be fooled into believing these are natural voices.

For contrast, select the **Plus** tab and listen to the available samples. While there are subtle tells that suggest these aren't quite natural voices, the casual listener would be excused for believing these are actual recordings of people reading a script.

Now, it's time to experiment with different text samples. Start with a simple paragraph from your favorite novel or an article you're interested in. Copy the text and paste or type it into the NaturalReader text window, then press the play button. Choose different voices for the same text sample, to hear the breadth of options available.

For a deeper dive, take advantage of NaturalReader's ability to handle different types of content. Try typing in a poem, an excerpt from a technical manual, or even a recipe. Notice how the software adjusts the delivery to suit the content type, emphasizing key points in an instructional text or capturing the rhythm in poetry. This flexibility makes NaturalReader a versatile tool, whether you're using it for leisure, study, or work. By exploring these variations, you not only enhance your experience but also gain insights into how AI can enrich content consumption through auditory means.

Getting Started with Text-to-Music

Picture a quiet room suddenly filled with melodies conjured from mere words. This is the realm of text-to-music (TTM) models, where text prompts transform into harmonious compositions. Models like Riffusion, Suno AI, and Udio are at the forefront of this innovation, each bringing a unique approach to music generation.

Riffusion stands out for its ability to create varied styles by interpreting text as musical prompts. It leverages neural networks trained on diverse music datasets to produce compositions that can evoke different emotions, from the upbeat to the melancholic.

Suno AI focuses on generating ambient and atmospheric tracks, perfect for background scores or meditative experiences. It excels in producing seamless loops, allowing sounds to flow without interruption.

Udio, meanwhile, offers a more experimental approach, embracing avant-garde styles and unexpected musical patterns, making it a favorite among creators seeking something out of the ordinary.

Training TTM models requires a nuanced understanding of both language and music. These models are trained using vast libraries of music paired with descriptive text, allowing them to learn the relationship between words and sounds. They analyze patterns in the music, such as rhythm, melody, and harmony, and correlate these with textual descriptions. This process enables them to generate music that aligns with the emotional and thematic intent of the text.

While similar to text-to-speech models in their reliance on natural language processing, TTM models differ in their focus on musical elements. They must balance linguistic understanding with musical creativity, a challenging task that combines art and technology.

As powerful as these tools are, they also have limitations. Riffusion may struggle with highly complex compositions, while Suno AI might lack the dynamism needed for more energetic tracks. Udio's experimental focus can result in output that's too avant-garde for traditional tastes.

Free versions of TTM models often provide limited access to features, restricting the complexity and length of compositions. Paid subscriptions unlock advanced capabilities, such as higher quality audio, more customization options, and access to exclusive sound libraries. For those who frequently use TTM for professional projects or creative exploration, investing in a subscription can greatly enhance the quality and variety of the music produced.

Writing Your First Song

Creating music can be a thrilling experience. Riffusion makes this accessible even if you're not a seasoned musician. To start, you'll need to set up a free Riffusion account. Head over to their website, riffusion.com, and click **Start Creating→**. You'll need a Google or Discord account, or a mobile phone number to get started. Choose your login method and follow the instructions.

After submitting and verifying your information, you'll be prompted to accept Riffusion's terms of use. Click **Continue**, enter a unique user name, and you're ready to explore.

Once inside Riffusion, you'll find a user-friendly interface ready to assist you in crafting your first song. The platform offers various tools and settings designed to guide you through the creative process. You can go as simple or complex as you like.

To begin, try a simple prompt such as, **Give me a song that sounds like van Gogh's Starry Night feels**, then click **Generate**. In less than a minute, the Riffusion model will generate two entirely original songs, including lyrics and vocals.

Ready to try more? Click on the prompt bar and select the **Compose** tab. Here you can enter your own lyrics and select the musical settings you want. Choose a poem in the public domain from one of your favorite poets, such as Robert Burns. Or maybe you've written one yourself and want to hear it set to music.

Let's explore how to infuse your song with different styles and moods. Start by selecting a mood or theme for your composition. For instance, if you're aiming for an upbeat, energetic feel, you might use prompts like **sunny day at the beach** or **dancing under the stars**. These prompts help the AI understand the kind of atmosphere you're trying to create.

If a more melancholic tone suits your project, consider prompts such as **rainy afternoon solitude** or **lost in thought during twilight**.

These inputs guide the AI in selecting instruments, tempo, and melody that align with the mood you've envisioned.

When it comes to musical style, Riffusion offers a diverse palette to choose from. Experiment with genres by using prompts like **jazz-inspired evening lounge** or **folk tune with acoustic elements**.

Each genre brings unique characteristics, from the instruments used to the rhythm and harmony. You can further refine your song by adjusting the length. A short prompt like **30-second intro** focuses on creating impactful, concise segments, ideal for podcasts or video intros. Longer prompts, such as **3-minute ballad**, allow the AI to develop a more intricate and evolving composition, perfect for a standalone piece.

As you experiment, pay attention to the details Riffusion adds to your music. Listen to how the AI interprets your prompts, and don't hesitate to make adjustments. Maybe you want to increase the tempo for a livelier section or add an unexpected instrument to bring freshness to your tune. The platform's flexibility allows you to iterate and refine until you're satisfied with the final product.

As you grow more comfortable, try blending different styles and moods to see how they interact. Playing around with different options can lead to surprising and delightful results, broadening your creative horizons.

Key Takeaways

- Text-to-speech (TTS) technology converts written content into spoken audio, offering accessibility, convenience, and creative utility—distinct from traditional audiobooks, which are voiced by human actors under licensed publishing agreements.

- TTS models are trained with natural language processing (NLP) techniques to generate lifelike speech, emphasizing pronunciation, cadence, and emotion across a wide range of voices and languages.

- Text-to-music (TTM) models like Riffusion, Suno AI, and Udio translate descriptive prompts into unique audio compositions, enabling users to generate background music or artistic pieces based on emotion, mood, or genre.

- Creating music with TTM tools is intuitive and expressive, allowing for experimentation with mood, genre, and rhythm—even without traditional musical training.

Chapter 8

—

Going Farther with AI

I n the preceding chapters, we've explored not only what AI is, but how to use it for your own creative and professional pursuits. It would be impossible in a single book to list all the ways AI can enhance your life, but as we close out Part 2, I want to present you with some areas for deeper exploration, as well as a few words of caution.

Build Your Tech Skills with AI

The AI landscape evolves at a breathtaking pace, and staying current requires curiosity, consistency, and a willingness to experiment. Fortunately, you don't need to become a computer scientist to keep up. With the right habits and tools, anyone can continue building AI fluency well beyond these pages.

One of the simplest yet most powerful ways to grow your skills is by using AI regularly in everyday life. Whether you're planning meals, organizing your schedule, drafting emails, or brainstorming your next big idea, the more you practice giving thoughtful prompts and refining results, the more confident and creative you'll become. Treat every interaction with AI as a mini learning experience. What worked? What didn't? How could your prompt have been clearer or more creative? This self-reflection builds skill faster than any formal lesson.

You can also follow AI news and updates through curated newsletters and websites like *The Rundown AI*, *Ben's Bites*, or *Import AI*. These sources deliver digestible updates on new tools, research, and best practices. Consider subscribing to a few and setting aside five minutes a day to scan headlines. Over time, you'll develop a sense of where the field is headed and which innovations are most relevant to your goals.

To go deeper, explore free and paid online courses. Platforms like Coursera, Udemy, and LinkedIn Learning offer practical introductions to prompt engineering, automation, or even no-code app building. Some courses are designed for non-technical users and focus on real-world skills like automating tasks with Zapier, designing AI art portfolios, or using chatbots to support a small business.

Another valuable approach is to join communities where AI enthusiasts gather. Spaces like Reddit's r/ChatGPT or Discord servers for tools like Midjourney and ElevenLabs are filled with discussions, prompt experiments, and collaborative projects. You'll learn a lot simply by observing what others are doing—and even more by asking questions or sharing your own creations. Community feedback can reveal insights you wouldn't discover on your own.

If you're interested in creating more advanced tools, consider learning basic scripting or automation using tools like Python, Make.com, or ChatGPT's built-in code interpreter. Even a small understanding of automation can unlock powerful workflows—whether that's auto-generating social media posts, summarizing emails, or building your own AI-powered productivity dashboard.

Finally, adopt a mindset of lifelong exploration. New models, tools, and interfaces are released constantly. Instead of waiting for a perfect roadmap, allow yourself to play. Test new apps. Compare different models. Build something messy, and refine it later. The goal isn't mastery—it's motion. Each small project, each new prompt, is a stepping stone toward deeper confidence and capability.

By reading this book, you've already taken the first big step. Now it's time to apply what you've learned, stay curious, and keep building. The world of AI is still being written—and with the skills you've developed here, you're now one of its co-authors.

A Word about Rights

Think of intellectual property rights as the keys to safeguarding your creative and innovative endeavors. These rights span a wide range of protections designed to ensure that creators can control and benefit from their inventions, artistic works, and brands.

At the heart of intellectual property, or IP, are four main categories: patents, copyrights, trademarks, and trade secrets. Each serves a distinct purpose. Patents protect inventions and processes, granting inventors exclusive rights over their creations for a set amount of time. Copyrights apply to original works of authorship, such as books, music, and software, allowing creators to control how their works are used. Trademarks protect symbols, names, and slogans used to identify goods and services, preventing confusion among consumers. Lastly, trade secrets involve confidential business information that provides a competitive edge, like the secret formula for a beloved soft drink or a blend of herbs and spices.

As we explore the realm of artificial intelligence, the intersection of AI and intellectual property becomes increasingly complex. When AI systems generate content, questions arise, such as, Who owns the rights to these creations?

Traditional IP laws were crafted with human inventors and authors in mind, posing challenges in assigning rights to AI-generated works. For instance, patent laws typically require a human inventor, complicating matters when AI-driven innovations emerge. Similarly, copyright laws imply the need for a human author, raising questions about the protectability of AI-generated art or music. This gray area in IP law leaves developers and users navigating uncharted waters, seeking clarity on who can claim ownership and control over AI-generated content.

In the United States, the current legal framework does not recognize AI as an inventor or author, meaning AI-generated works may not qualify for protection under traditional IP laws. Instead, the focus is on the human involvement in the creation process. If a human actively guides the AI and contributes creatively, they may hold the rights to the resulting work.

However, when AI operates autonomously, the situation becomes more ambiguous, leading to debates about whether these works fall into the public domain or belong to the entity that owns the AI system. This uncertainty extends to other jurisdictions, each grappling with how to adapt existing IP laws to accommodate AI's capabilities.

Globally, attitudes toward AI and IP rights vary. In the European Union, the focus is on ensuring that AI-generated works involve significant human input to qualify for copyright protection. This aligns with the belief that creativity stems from human expression and originality. Meanwhile, countries like China are exploring the potential for granting IP rights to AI-generated works, reflecting their commitment to encouraging innovation and technological advancement.

The United Kingdom and Ukraine have introduced specific provisions that recognize AI-generated content under certain conditions, acknowledging the evolving landscape of AI creation. These differing approaches highlight the ongoing debate about the role of AI in creative processes and the appropriate allocation of rights.

As AI continues to change and grow, so too will the legal frameworks that govern intellectual property. Stakeholders, including developers, businesses, and policymakers, must engage in discussions to shape these frameworks, balancing innovation with the protection of creators' rights.

For developers and users of AI technologies, understanding IP rights is crucial to navigating the legal landscape and ensuring compliance. This includes keeping informed about changes in legislation, seeking legal advice when needed, and considering the implications of IP rights when developing or using AI systems. By doing so, we can foster an environment where AI enhances human creativity without undermining the rights of those who contribute to its development.

In this rapidly changing world, the intersection of AI and intellectual property presents both challenges and opportunities. As we explore the possibilities AI offers, it's essential to remain mindful of the rights and responsibilities that come with it. By acknowledging the nuances of IP rights and adapting to the developing legal landscape, we can help ensure that AI serves as a tool for innovation while respecting the contributions of human creators.

Reading the Fine Print

Navigating the digital landscape often involves dealing with service provider terms of service, a daunting task for many. These terms are essentially agreements between you and the service provider outlining how you can use their platform, what you can expect in terms of service, and your rights and responsibilities. They are designed to protect both the provider and the user, ensuring a mutual understanding of the platform's use.

However, these documents can be lengthy and filled with legal jargon, making them difficult to digest. Yet, understanding them is crucial because, once you agree, you are legally bound by their terms. Ignoring them might lead to unintended breaches that could limit your access or lead to more severe legal consequences.

When we compare the terms of service of the platforms discussed in the previous chapters, we find both commonalities and differences. For instance, platforms like ChatGPT and DALL·E, operated by OpenAI, have detailed terms that cover everything from data usage to content ownership. OpenAI's terms emphasize that while they provide access to powerful AI tools, users are responsible for ensuring their inputs and outputs comply with applicable laws. This includes having due regard for privacy rights and making sure that generated content doesn't infringe on intellectual property rights.

On the other hand, platforms like Canva and Adobe Sensei offer terms that focus more on the creative freedoms of users while outlining the limits of liability and the importance of adhering to copyright laws. These platforms allow for a broader scope of creative expression but remind users to respect the intellectual property of others. Understanding these nuances can help you use these platforms effectively and ethically.

Ownership of prompts and outputs on these platforms can be a complex issue. In most cases, you, as the user, retain ownership of the inputs you provide. However, the outputs, especially those generated by AI, may have different rules.

For instance, OpenAI's terms state that users generally own the outputs generated by models like ChatGPT and DALL·E, provided they comply with the terms of service. This means that while you can use and distribute the content, you must ensure it doesn't violate any laws or third-party rights.

Similarly, Adobe Sensei allows users to own their creative outputs, but with a caveat: the responsibility of ensuring no infringement on existing copyrights lies with the user. This ownership model empowers you to utilize AI creatively while maintaining accountability.

To illustrate how users can leverage these outputs, consider a few examples. Suppose you create a unique image using DALL·E for a marketing campaign. You can legally use this image across various platforms, provided it adheres to copyright laws and doesn't replicate existing works. Similarly, if you generate text content using ChatGPT, you might use it for blog posts, articles, or even as part of a book, as long as the content remains original and non-infringing.

In the realm of design, leveraging Canva or Adobe Sensei to craft striking visuals for presentations or promotional material is common practice. These outputs can enhance business communications, drive engagement, and support branding efforts, offering a competitive edge in creative industries.

While exploring these possibilities, it's crucial to remain aware of the ethical responsibilities tied to content creation. The allure of AI-generated content is its ease and efficiency, but it should not replace human oversight in ensuring accuracy and originality. Users must regularly check for plagiarism, respect privacy, and ensure that their AI-generated outputs do not perpetuate biased or harmful narratives. By maintaining this ethical vigilance, you can maximize the benefits of AI tools while contributing positively to the digital ecosystem.

Understanding and navigating terms of service, ownership rules, and ethical considerations may seem daunting, but they are integral to leveraging AI's full potential responsibly. By reading the fine print, you empower yourself to use these platforms effectively, ensuring that your creativity and innovation remain protected and respected in the digital age.

Key Takeaways

- Continual learning is essential to thrive in the fast-moving AI space—regular use, prompt experimentation, and curiosity are key.

- Online courses and tutorials offer accessible paths for learning prompt engineering, automation, and no-code app building.

- Intellectual property (IP) laws are evolving to keep up with AI-generated content. Current protections focus on human-guided contributions.

- Terms of service agreements define how AI platforms can be used, what rights you retain, and where responsibility lies for legal compliance. Users typically own their prompts and outputs, but must ensure that generated content complies with copyright and ethical standards.

Part 3
—
Thriving with AI

Chapter 9

—

Building Your First AI Tool

I f you've made it this far—diving deep into the history and development of AI as a science, then kicking the tires on some of the amazing tools available for average users to leverage the power of AI—then *Congratulations!* It's safe to say that you are no longer a beginner.

You can stop right here, put down the book, and explore the tools you've already discovered. Just this much will open up new opportunities and areas of exploration and expression that can deeply enrich your life for years to come.

But if you want to dive deeper, to explore how you can personalize your AI tools and fine-tune them to better support your work and home life, then let's keep going.

Before We Start

This exercise can only be completed on a computer (Windows–, macOS–, or Linux-based)—it will not work on tablets or your smartphone. It may get pretty technical, and you'll be poking under the hood of your computer's operating system. Don't worry—we won't break anything. And while no coding knowledge is required, we will be building code-based tools, but I'll guide you step by step through the work.

Because we'll be working with object recognition, you will also need a camera to feed images to the model. If your computer has a built-in camera, that will work just fine. Otherwise, you'll need to use a digital camera connected by USB.

Because of its complexity, I recommend setting aside an hour or so to do this all in one block so you don't lose your place. While we're a step above Beginner, we're a long way from Mastery. Even so, this should give you a taste of what you can build on your own with the help of AI.

Ready? Let's go.

Hands-On Exercise: Your First AI Tool

In this guide, you'll learn how to set up and train a real-time object detection system using PyTorch, OpenCV, and a pre-trained YOLOv5 model. The system will use your webcam to detect objects live.

This exercise will require you to copy code (programming language) into your terminal environment to instruct the system on how to work. Line numbers are shown for reference only and should not be included in your code. You can copy the code straight from the book or—to help avoid typos and errors—you can find the code on our website at adbooks.pub/resources.

Now, be aware that software is continually being updated, compatibilities change, and so on. We can't guarantee that what worked at the time of writing this will still work without issues by the time you read it. If something doesn't seem to work or you get stuck in the process, remember your AI friend ChatGPT and use it to help you move forward.

Step 1: Install Python on Your Computer

Python is a high-level, versatile programming language popular for its simplicity and readability. It is often used in web development, data science, automation, artificial intelligence, and more due to its extensive libraries and ease of use. To install the root program on your computer:

- Using your web browser, visit https://www.python.org/downloads.

- The browser should recognize which operating system you're working on and automatically provide the correct download prompt. Otherwise, select your operating system (e.g., Windows, macOS, Linux) and download the appropriate version of the current release of Python. (Remember where you save the download.)

- Once the download is complete, locate and run the file. On Windows, be sure to check the options to "Use admin privileges when installing py.exe" and "Add python.exe to PATH." This will avoid headaches later. Once you've checked these, click on **Install**.

When the Python installation is complete, feel free to explore some of the tutorials and documentation, or simply click **Close** and continue to the next step.

Step 2: Install PyTorch on Your Computer

Now we're going to get into the weeds a bit. PyTorch is an open-source machine learning framework developed by Meta (Facebook), designed for deep learning applications, including neural networks and AI research. It provides dynamic computation graphs, GPU acceleration, and an intuitive Pythonic interface, making it a popular choice for research, prototyping, and production deployment in AI and data science.

In order to use PyTorch, we'll need to call it through a Python script, which will require entering instructions in the system Terminal. If you're familiar with the Terminal on your operating system, you're well ahead of the curve. Feel free to jump right down to the PyTorch installation instructions. Otherwise, let's go through a brief tutorial on what it is and how to use it.

The Terminal (or command line) is a text-based interface used to interact with your computer's operating system. Instead of clicking through graphical menus, you type commands to navigate files, run programs, manage processes, and configure system settings. It provides direct access to system functions, making it a versatile and effective tool for developers, system administrators, and advanced users.

The Terminal is available on all major operating systems: Linux and macOS use Unix-based shells like Bash (Bourne Again Shell) or Zsh, while

Windows offers Command Prompt (cmd.exe) and PowerShell, with the option to install a Unix-like terminal via WSL (Windows Subsystem for Linux).

To use the Terminal, open it from your system's applications or shortcut keys (**Ctrl+Alt+T** on Linux, **Cmd+Space → Terminal** on macOS, **Win+R → cmd** on Windows). You'll then enter the commands as simple text. Syntax rules are very specific, so be sure to enter the commands exactly as shown or copy and paste them from our online resources (link above).

Crystal clear? Or clear as mud? Don't worry—it'll all make sense as we go.

- Open your system terminal as described above.

- Confirm that Python is correctly installed by entering

```
python --version
```

If you don't get a response like **Python 3.12.1**, then go through the installation process described above.

- Install PyTorch and its dependencies. This step may take some time, so be patient.

```
pip install torch torchvision opencv-python numpy matplotlib ultralytics
```

- If you receive any notifications of available updates, go ahead and follow the on-screen instructions.

Step 3: Download the YOLOv5 Pre-Trained Model

- Clone the YOLOv5 model from the GitHub repository:

```
git clone https://github.com/ultralytics/yolov5.git
cd yolov5
```

- Next, install YOLOv5's dependencies:

```
pip install -r requirements.txt
```

Step 4: Run Real-Time Object Detection

Now that PyTorch and the YOLOv5 model are installed, we can write a Python script to enable AI-powered object detection on your computer. On Windows machines, we'll use Notepad. On macOS/Linux, you can use the Terminal text editor called Nano.

- In Windows, enter: **notepad realtime_detection.py**. If prompted to create a new file, click **Yes**.

- On macOS/Linux, enter: **nano realtime_detection.py**.

- Copy the following code into your text editor.

```python
import torch
import cv2
import numpy as np
from ultralytics import YOLO

# Load YOLOv5 model (pre-trained on COCO dataset)
model = YOLO("yolov5s.pt")

# Open webcam
cap = cv2.VideoCapture(0)  # 0 for default webcam
while cap.isOpened():
    ret, frame = cap.read()
    if not ret:
        break

# Convert frame from BGR to RGB
rgb_frame = cv2.cvtColor(frame, cv2.COLOR_BGR2RGB)

# Run object detection
results = model(rgb_frame)

# Draw bounding boxes
for r in results:
    for box in r.boxes:
```

```
        x1, y1, x2, y2 = (
            box.xyxy[0].cpu().numpy().astype(int)
        )
        conf = box.conf[0].cpu().numpy()
        cls = int(box.cls[0].cpu().numpy())
        if conf > 0.5:  # Confidence threshold
        label = f"{model.names[cls]}: {conf:.2f}"
        cv2.rectangle(
            frame,
            (x1, y1),
            (x2, y2),
            (0, 255, 0),
            2
        )
        cv2.putText(
            frame,
            label,
            (x1, y1 - 10),
            cv2.FONT_HERSHEY_SIMPLEX,
            0.5,
            (0, 255, 0),
            2
        )

# Display output
cv2.imshow("YOLOv5 Real-Time Detection", frame)

# Exit when 'q' is pressed
if cv2.waitKey(1) & 0xFF == ord("q"):
    break
    cap.release()
    cv2.destroyAllWindows()
```

Now, you can save the file and close the editor.

- In Windows: Click on **File → Close Tab** (or **Ctrl+W**). When prompted to save changes, click **Save**.

- In macOS/Linux (nano): Enter **Cmd+X** or **Ctrl+X**. Enter **Y** to save changes. Press **Enter** to confirm the file name.

Return to the Terminal (if you're not already there) and run the script:

```
python realtime_detection.py
```

This will call the YOLOv5 model and start the object-detection routine. It may take quite some time to initialize the program, but once it starts you should see a video window with object identification active.

When you're through being amazed, press **q** to exit the program. (If that doesn't work, try **Ctrl+C** or **Cmd+C**).

Key Takeaways

- Using the system Terminal (or Command Prompt/PowerShell on Windows) allows you to install dependencies, manage files, and execute Python scripts efficiently.

- Pre-assembled code packages and pre-trained AI models can be called and executed with minimal coding required on the part of the end user.

- AI software evolves, so you are encouraged to troubleshoot issues and seek AI assistance (e.g., ChatGPT) for solutions when things don't work as expected.

Chapter 10

—

Future-Proofing Your Career

I n a workplace alive with data and automation, professionals who harness AI don't just adapt—they lead.

Whether in finance, marketing, education, or healthcare, those fluent in AI tools are shaping tomorrow's industries. This chapter shows how to develop the skills that keep you relevant, resilient, and ready for what's next.

And, don't worry—I promised you could master the tools presented in this book even if you're not tech-savvy, and that's true. But, if you have some prompt engineering or coding skills, or if you're interested in developing them, the following information will give you an extra boost.

AI Competencies Employers Look For

Employers across various industries are increasingly on the lookout for individuals who possess specific AI-related skills. Among the most sought-after is proficiency in programming languages such as R and Python. These languages are foundational in AI development due to their versatility and extensive libraries tailored for data science and machine learning.

Python, with its simple syntax, allows for the rapid development of AI models, making it a favorite among developers and data scientists. R, renowned for its statistical prowess, is invaluable for data analysis, enabling the creation of detailed visualizations that inform decision-making. Mastery of these languages is crucial for code developers getting started in the AI space, as they provide the tools necessary to build and implement AI tools that can unravel challenging problems and enhance business operations.

Beyond programming, a deep understanding of machine learning algorithms and frameworks is essential. Machine learning, a subset of AI, involves working with models to enable them to recognize patterns and make predictions based on data. Familiarity with popular frameworks like TensorFlow and PyTorch allows professionals to construct, train, and deploy models efficiently. These frameworks support a broad range of applications, from NLP to image recognition, and their open-source nature encourages continuous learning and innovation.

Recognizing the right algorithm for a given problem and adapting models to fit specific needs are skills that set candidates apart in the competitive job market. As AI technology develops, staying aware of the latest advancements in these frameworks ensures that professionals remain at the forefront of innovation.

Equally important is the ability to analyze and interpret large datasets, a skill that underpins all AI endeavors. Data is the lifeblood of AI, and the ability to sort through huge amounts of information to extract meaningful insights is invaluable. Employers seek individuals who can not only manage data but also derive actionable intelligence from it. This involves understanding data preprocessing techniques, identifying biases, and ensuring data quality.

Visualization tools, such as Tableau or Power BI, play a big part in presenting data insights in a clear and compelling manner. By transforming raw data into visual narratives, professionals can communicate findings effectively, driving strategic decision-making and innovation within their organizations.

The demand for these competencies isn't confined to tech companies alone. Industries such as healthcare, finance, and manufacturing are increasingly integrating AI into their processes. In healthcare, AI assists in diagnostics and personalized medicine, while in finance, it enhances fraud detection and risk management. Manufacturing firms leverage AI for predictive maintenance and optimizing supply chains.

This cross-industry adoption underscores the versatility of AI skills and their potential to revolutionize traditional business models. As organizations work through the complexities of digital transformation, they rely on skilled professionals who can span the gap between technology and business strategy.

The growing emphasis on AI competencies has led to a surge in AI-related job postings. Positions like data scientists, machine learning engineers, and AI specialists are becoming more and more common. They often command competitive salaries due to high demand.

As companies recognize the transformative power of AI, they invest in building teams equipped with the necessary skills to harness this technology effectively. This trend is reflected in educational initiatives, with courses and certifications in AI becoming increasingly available on platforms like Coursera and Udemy. These resources provide flexible learning opportunities, enabling professionals to improve their skillsets and adapt to the evolving requirements of the workforce.

To ensure a successful career in an AI-driven world, it's important to cultivate a mindset of continuous learning and adaptability. The pace of technological advancement means that AI tools and techniques are constantly evolving. Professionals who remain curious and open to learning new skills will find themselves well-positioned to capitalize on emerging opportunities.

To further explore the AI skills that employers are seeking, consider engaging in self-assessment exercises that help identify areas for improvement and growth. This reflective approach encourages a proactive attitude toward skill development, ensuring that you remain competitive in the job market.

Self-Assessment Exercise: Evaluating Your AI Competencies

Instructions: Reflect on the following questions and consider how your existing skillset aligns with the industry's needs. This exercise is designed to help you identify strengths and areas for development.

1. **Programming Proficiency:** How comfortable are you with programming languages like Python and R? Can you build and deploy basic machine learning models?

2. **Understanding of Machine Learning:** Do you have experience working with frameworks like TensorFlow or PyTorch? How familiar are you with different machine learning algorithms?

3. **Data Analysis Skills:** Can you effectively analyze and interpret large datasets? Are you proficient in using data visualization tools to communicate insights?

4. **Ongoing Learning:** How do you stay updated on AI trends and technologies? Do you actively look for new opportunities to learn and grow?

5. **Cross-Industry Applications:** How have you applied AI skills in different industries? Can you identify potential areas where AI could enhance business processes?

Use your responses to guide your professional development and explore resources that can help strengthen your AI competencies. This self-assessment is a starting point for crafting your personalized learning plan to align with your career aspirations and the evolving demands of the AI landscape.

Future-Proof Skills for an AI-Driven World

The evolving AI landscape rewards professionals who can adapt and thrive amidst constant technological change. One of the most critical abilities in this new era is adaptability, the capacity to adjust your mindset and methods in response to new AI tools and technologies. As we witness rapid advancements, the workplace transforms almost overnight. New AI applications appear regularly, offering enhanced capabilities that can redefine job roles.

To stay relevant in a rapidly developing workplace, you must embrace change, learning to navigate unfamiliar tools with ease. Shift your viewpoint to recognize challenges as opportunities for growth rather than obstacles. This flexibility will allow you to pivot as needed, ensuring that you remain a valuable asset in any professional setting.

Continuous learning and upskilling are equally vital in maintaining relevance. The AI field is dynamic, with innovations emerging at a pace that can quickly make yesterday's knowledge obsolete. Engaging in lifelong learning means actively seeking new information and tools to keep pace with these changes. This might involve taking online courses, attending workshops, or participating in webinars to deepen your understanding of AI technologies and their applications.

Upskilling is not a simple, single event but an ongoing process. It requires dedication and curiosity to explore new domains and technologies. By committing to continuous learning, you cultivate a competitive advantage and position yourself as a forward-thinking professional capable of leveraging AI advancements to drive innovation and efficiency.

In addition to technical skills, developing strong analytical and critical thinking abilities is crucial. As AI systems become more enmeshed with business processes, the ability to interpret data and make informed decisions becomes increasingly important. You must learn to analyze trends, assess risks, and evaluate the impact of AI solutions on organizational goals.

This analytical mindset will help you navigate complex problems and devise strategic solutions that align with business objectives. Moreover, critical thinking enables you to question assumptions and challenge conventional wisdom, fostering innovation and creativity in your approach to problem-solving.

Communication skills also play a pivotal role in the AI-driven world. As AI systems generate huge amounts of data and insights, the ability to communicate these findings effectively to diverse audiences is essential. This requires not only technical proficiency but also the ability to reduce complex ideas into clear, actionable insights.

Whether presenting to stakeholders, collaborating with cross-functional teams, or educating clients, strong communication skills will help you convey the value of AI solutions and drive successful implementation. Additionally, effective communication fosters collaboration and teamwork, ensuring that AI initiatives work in concert with organizational goals and deliver tangible benefits.

Interpersonal skills are equally important in an AI-driven workplace. As AI automates routine tasks, human roles increasingly focus on strategic and creative endeavors. Building strong relationships, collaborating across teams, and fostering a culture of innovation become paramount.

By developing empathy and emotional intelligence, you can navigate complex interpersonal dynamics and build trust and rapport with colleagues and clients. These skills enhance your ability to lead and inspire others, driving collective efforts toward achieving organizational goals. In a world where human interaction remains irreplaceable, cultivating interpersonal skills will ensure you thrive in any professional setting.

Furthermore, an understanding of ethical considerations in AI deployment is crucial. As AI systems influence decision-making processes, ethical implications must be considered. This involves ensuring transparency, fairness, and accountability in AI applications. You should be aware of potential biases in data and algorithms, and strive to develop solutions that promote equity and inclusivity.

In adopting an ethical mindset, you contribute to responsible AI development, building trust with stakeholders and ensuring positive societal impact. This awareness positions you as a leader in ethical AI practices, capable of guiding organizations toward sustainable and responsible innovation.

Thriving in an AI-driven world requires a diverse skill set that encompasses technical proficiency, adaptability, continuous learning, analytical thinking, communication, interpersonal skills, and ethical awareness. By developing these competencies, you position yourself as a valuable asset in any industry, equipped to navigate the challenges of a rapidly changing workplace. Embracing these skills will not only future-proof your career but also empower you to add meaningful contributions to the advancement of AI technologies and their positive impact on society.

Preparing for AI-Enhanced Job Roles

In today's fast-changing job market, the integration of AI across various sectors has created a plethora of new opportunities. To thrive in this complex world, it's important to understand the emerging roles that AI is enhancing and transforming.

Begin by exploring the current trends affecting your industry to identify where AI is making the most significant impact. Look for industry reports, articles, and job postings that highlight the skills and roles in demand. By staying informed, you can pinpoint positions that not only interest you but also leverage AI in innovative ways.

Networking with professionals already working in AI-driven roles can provide helpful new insights and guidance for your career path. Go to seminars and industry conferences where experts talk about the latest advancements and their implications for the workforce. These gatherings give you the opportunity to engage in conversations with like-minded individuals and broaden your understanding of the market dynamics.

As you identify AI-enhanced roles that align with your career goals, the next step is to create a portfolio that effectively showcases your practical AI skills and projects. A well-crafted portfolio is a tangible expression of your abilities, highlighting your competence in applying AI to solve real-world problems.

Start by choosing a wide range of projects that demonstrate your expertise and versatility. Include projects that span different aspects of AI, such as machine learning, NLP, or computer vision. Each project should be accompanied by clear documentation that outlines the problem statement, methodologies used, and results achieved. Highlight the impact of your work using data-driven metrics to showcase improvements or gains. Additionally, consider including personal reflections on the challenges faced and lessons learned during each project. This not only demonstrates your problem-solving skills but also your ability to adapt and grow.

Collaborating on open-source projects can further enrich your portfolio, showcasing your teamwork skills and code quality. Contributing to the AI community through blog posts, articles, or presentations can position you as a thought leader, enhancing your credibility and visibility in the field.

Tailoring your skillset to meet the specific requirements of AI-enhanced roles involves a strategic approach. Begin by analyzing job descriptions for roles you aspire to and identifying the key skills and qualifications employers seek. This process will help you pinpoint areas where you may need additional training or experience.

Consider enrolling in relevant courses, workshops, or certification programs to bridge any skill gaps. Online platforms offer a plethora of resources that support various learning styles and schedules, making it easier than ever to upskill. As you acquire new knowledge, seek opportunities to apply it in practical settings, such as internships, freelance projects, or volunteer work. These experiences not only enhance your skills but also provide valuable networking opportunities and industry exposure.

An important step is to tailor your cover letter and resume so that they highlight your AI skills and experiences. Use specific language and examples that align with the job requirements, demonstrating your ability to contribute effectively to the organization. Highlight your accomplishments with AI projects, emphasizing how they relate to the goals of the prospective employer.

Successfully navigating interviews for AI-enhanced positions requires careful preparation and a focus on both technical and behavioral aspects. For technical interviews, familiarize yourself with common questions related to AI concepts, algorithms, and programming languages. Practice coding challenges and problem-solving exercises to demonstrate your proficiency in real-time scenarios.

Reviewing your portfolio projects and being able to discuss them confidently is crucial. Be prepared to explain the methodologies you used, the obstacles you faced, and the outcomes you achieved. This will not only demonstrate your technical expertise but highlights your ability to communicate complex ideas clearly.

Behavioral interviews are designed to gauge your soft skills and cultural fit within the organization. Prepare by reflecting on past experiences that highlight your adaptability, teamwork, and problem-solving abilities. Use the STAR method (Situation, Task, Action, Result) to frame your responses, providing concrete examples of how you have navigated challenges and contributed to team success.

Understanding the company's mission and values is also essential. Crafting your responses to align with their goals and vision shows you possess a genuine interest and commitment to the role.

In addition to traditional interview preparations, consider the growing trend of AI-driven interviews. Companies are increasingly using AI to assess candidates, analyzing verbal and vocal data to evaluate responses. Preparing for these interviews involves practicing how to articulate your thoughts clearly and confidently.

Focus on using relevant keywords from the job description, as AI tools may rank candidates based on these criteria. Conduct mock interviews with peers or use AI-based interview simulators to refine your responses and gain feedback. Remember to maintain a professional demeanor, dressing appropriately and maintaining eye contact with the camera. By preparing thoroughly for AI-enhanced job roles, you position yourself as a strong candidate ready to thrive in the evolving landscape.

As you navigate this dynamic environment, remember that the journey doesn't end with securing a role. Continuous growth and adaptation are essential to thriving in an AI-enhanced career. Stay engaged with the AI community, keep abreast of emerging trends, and seek opportunities to expand your skillset.

Embrace change as an opportunity for growth, and remain open to new challenges. This proactive mindset will not only future-proof your career but also enable you to make meaningful contributions to the development of AI applications and their positive impact on society.

Understanding the job market, building a strong portfolio, tailoring your skills, and mastering interviews are crucial steps in preparing for AI-enhanced roles. They position you for success in this dynamic landscape.

Key Takeaways

- AI skills are growing in demand across industries, especially programming (Python, R), machine learning, and data analysis.

- The ability to continually adapt and learn new skills is critical for staying relevant in an AI-driven job market.

- Soft skills—including communication, interpersonal, and ethical awareness—are as important as technical expertise.

- A strong portfolio and interview preparation can set you apart in AI-enhanced job roles.

Chapter 11

—

Continuous AI Learning

You sit in a bustling café with a group of like-minded professionals huddled around laptops, sipping coffee, and discussing the latest AI trends. You're not just keeping up with the digital age, you're thriving in it. This is the spirit of continuous learning in AI—a dynamic field where staying updated is not just advantageous but essential.

Time Management for Busy Learners

Embarking on an AI learning journey requires more than just enthusiasm. It demands a strategic approach to time management. Setting clear and achievable learning objectives is the first step. Consider what you aim to accomplish, whether it's mastering a specific AI tool or understanding a complex concept. Break these objectives into smaller, manageable tasks. For instance, if your goal is to learn machine learning, you might begin by focusing on understanding the basics of algorithms before tackling more advanced topics. This approach not only clarifies your path but also provides a sense of accomplishment as you progress through each milestone.

Organizing your study time effectively is another critical aspect. Start by assessing your weekly schedule to find blocks of time that can be dedicated to learning. Consistency is key, so aim to allocate regular, uninterrupted periods for study.

If you're juggling multiple responsibilities, consider integrating AI learning into existing routines. For example, listen to AI-related podcasts during your daily commute or review course materials during lunch breaks. This integration transforms potential downtime into productive learning moments, maximizing the use of your time.

Microlearning is an approach that aligns well with busy schedules. It involves consuming educational content in short, focused bursts rather than lengthy sessions. This method enables you to absorb information quickly and retain it more effectively. For instance, dedicate 10 to 15 minutes each day to learning a new AI concept. Over time, these small increments add up, leading to substantial progress. Microlearning not only fits seamlessly into hectic lifestyles but also keeps your engagement high, preventing burnout from prolonged study sessions.

To support your time management efforts, consider using digital tools and apps designed to boost productivity and organization. Apps like Todoist and Trello offer features to help you track tasks, set reminders, and prioritize objectives. These tools enable you to visualize your learning journey, breaking down complex projects into actionable steps.

Additionally, calendar apps like Google Calendar can be invaluable for scheduling dedicated study periods and setting reminders for important deadlines. By leveraging technology, you can streamline your learning process and maintain focus amid the demands of daily life.

Furthermore, tools like Forbes' recommended time management apps offer additional resources for optimizing your schedule. These apps provide features such as task prioritization, time tracking, and integration with other productivity tools. By exploring different options, you can identify the tools that best suit your preferences and learning style, ensuring a personalized approach to managing your time.

As you delve deeper into AI, the importance of setting boundaries becomes evident. Allocate specific times for learning and stick to them, minimizing distractions during these periods. Communicate your schedule to family or colleagues to establish a supportive environment. This boundary-setting not only enhances concentration but also fosters a culture of respect for your learning commitments.

Finally, reflect regularly on your progress. Set aside time to evaluate which strategies are working and where you might need to make adjustments. Are you meeting your learning objectives? Is your schedule realistic and sustainable?

By assessing your approach, you can make informed decisions, optimizing your time management and ensuring continuous growth. Embrace the flexibility to change your approach as needed, keeping your learning journey aligned with changing circumstances and goals.

Online AI Courses Worth Exploring

In the arena of artificial intelligence, the wealth of online courses offers an unparalleled opportunity to learn and grow, regardless of where you are or what your background might be. These courses come in various formats and levels, catering to both the curious beginner and the seasoned professional seeking to refine their skills. The flexibility of online learning means you can adjust your education plan to align with your schedule, helping you to integrate AI study into your life without sacrificing other commitments.

When selecting a course, consider what you want to achieve. Are you looking to gain a broad understanding of AI principles, or are you aiming to specialize in a particular area, such as machine learning or natural language processing? Your goals will guide you toward courses that align with your aspirations.

For those starting their AI exploration, beginner-friendly courses offer a solid foundation without overwhelming technical jargon. Coursera, for example, provides *AI For Everyone* by DeepLearning.AI, which demystifies AI concepts and their applications in a non-technical manner. This course is perfect for anyone curious about AI's impact on society and businesses, without delving into the complexities of coding and algorithms. It emphasizes understanding AI's potential and limitations, preparing you to engage with AI discussions confidently. Courses like these are designed to spark interest and build a basic comprehension, setting the stage for more advanced study.

As you advance, courses that delve into technical aspects become invaluable. For those ready to dive deeper, *Introduction to Artificial Intelligence (AI)* by IBM, also available on Coursera, offers a comprehensive look at AI technologies. This course covers machine learning, neural networks, and AI applications across industries, providing hands-on experience with AI tools. Its structured approach provides a deep understanding of AI's building blocks, equipping you with the skills needed to develop and implement AI solutions. Interactive exercises and real-world examples reinforce learning, making complex topics accessible and engaging.

The format of online courses varies widely, from self-paced modules to instructor-led sessions with live interactions. Self-paced courses offer the advantage of flexibility, allowing you to learn at your own speed and revisit challenging concepts as needed. These courses often include video lectures, quizzes, and discussions, creating a comprehensive learning experience.

On the other hand, instructor-led courses provide a more guided approach, with opportunities for real-time feedback and collaboration with peers. This format fosters a sense of community, where you can communicate with instructors and fellow learners, sharing insights and solving problems together.

When evaluating courses, pay attention to the content coverage and depth. Confirm that the curriculum aligns with your learning goals and offers the level of detail you need. Some courses provide a broad overview of AI, touching on various topics without going into too much depth. These are ideal for gaining a general understanding and identifying areas of interest.

Others focus intensely on specific subjects, offering in-depth analysis and practical applications. These courses are suited for those who want to specialize or apply knowledge in real-world scenarios. Reading course reviews and syllabi can provide valuable insights into the course's comprehensiveness and relevance.

Choosing a course that fits your needs involves considering your current knowledge, goals, and available time. If you're a beginner, start with introductory courses that build a strong foundation. As you progress, select courses that challenge you and expand your expertise. Consider your career aspirations—whether you're aiming to become an AI engineer, data scientist, or product manager—and choose courses that align with these roles.

Many platforms, such as Coursera, also offer professional certificates upon completion, which can enhance your resume and open doors to new opportunities. These certificates signal to employers that you possess the skills and knowledge necessary to thrive in an AI-driven landscape.

When selecting courses, also consider the credentials of the instructors and the reputation of the institutions offering them. Courses taught by industry experts or renowned academics ensure that you're learning from those with deep insights and experience in the field.

Institutions like Stanford, MIT, and the University of Pennsylvania are known for their rigorous AI programs and contribute significantly to the field's advancement. Learning from such reputable sources not only enriches your understanding but also boosts your confidence in applying AI concepts in practical settings.

In addition to course content, pay attention to the learning resources provided. Quality courses often include supplementary materials such as readings, projects, and access to online communities. These resources enhance your learning experience, offering additional perspectives and opportunities for practical application.

Participating in forums or study groups can further enrich your understanding, allowing you to discuss ideas, ask questions, and gain insights from other students. This collaborative aspect of online learning mirrors real-world problem-solving, where diverse perspectives lead to innovative solutions.

Ultimately, the key to success in online AI courses lies in your commitment to learning and your willingness to explore new concepts. Approach each course with curiosity and an open mind, ready to engage with the material and apply what you learn.

The world of AI is vast and ever-evolving, offering endless opportunities for growth and discovery. By choosing the right courses and dedicating yourself to continuous learning, you position yourself to thrive in an AI-driven future, equipped with the knowledge and skills to make meaningful contributions to the field.

Staying Updated with AI Trends

In the ever-shifting landscape of artificial intelligence, staying informed about the latest advancements is crucial. The field evolves rapidly, with breakthroughs occurring across various domains. To keep abreast of these developments, you need access to reliable resources.

Start by following reputable tech news outlets that cover AI advancements regularly. Websites like TechCrunch and Wired offer insights into emerging technologies and innovations. Subscribing to AI-focused newsletters or podcasts can also provide curated updates that fit into your daily routine, making it easier to stay informed without feeling overwhelmed.

Academic research papers and publications are another valuable resource. They offer in-depth analysis and findings from cutting-edge studies, providing a glimpse into the future of AI. Platforms such as arXiv and

Google Scholar are treasure troves of scholarly articles, allowing you to explore a range of topics from machine learning algorithms to ethical considerations in AI. By engaging with academic research, you not only gain a deeper understanding of complex concepts but also cultivate a critical perspective on industry developments. Reading these papers regularly will sharpen your analytical skills and keep you at the forefront of AI knowledge.

Industry reports are equally important in understanding market trends and future directions. These reports often include data-driven insights and forecasts, helping you identify potential opportunities and challenges in the AI industry. Companies like McKinsey and Forrester publish annual reports that analyze AI's impact across various sectors, providing a comprehensive overview of its economic and social implications. Reviewing these reports keeps you informed about where AI is headed and what that means for your field or career. They also offer a glimpse into how companies are adopting AI and the innovations on the horizon.

To nurture a mindset of continuous learning and curiosity, it's essential to set aside dedicated time for regular updates. Allocate specific times each week to catch up on the latest news, research, and reports. This habit not only keeps you informed but also fosters a proactive approach to learning. Embrace this time as an opportunity to explore new ideas and technologies, pushing the boundaries of your knowledge. Curiosity is a driving force in the AI field, encouraging you to ask questions, seek answers, and remain open to new possibilities.

As new technologies and methodologies emerge, be willing to experiment and adapt. AI is a dynamic field where today's innovations might be tomorrow's standards. Embracing change means being open to learning new tools, techniques, and approaches.

For instance, if a new programming framework gains popularity, consider exploring it to understand its applications and advantages. This adaptability not only enhances your skill set but also prepares you for the inevitable shifts in the AI landscape. By remaining flexible, you position yourself to seize opportunities as they arise, ensuring your relevance in a fast-paced industry.

To support your growth, consider joining AI-focused communities or organizations. These groups often host webinars, workshops, and conferences where you can learn from experts and share your experiences. Participating in such events keeps you engaged with the AI community and provides a platform to exchange ideas. Whether it's a local AI meetup or an international conference, these gatherings offer valuable learning experiences that extend beyond traditional education. They also provide a sense of camaraderie, reminding you that you're part of a larger movement pushing the boundaries of technology.

Finally, remember that the path to mastering AI is a continuous one. The field is vast, with endless opportunities for exploration and discovery. As you stay updated with trends, remain curious and open-minded. Let your passion for learning guide you, and embrace the challenges and changes that come your way. In doing so, you'll not only keep pace with the evolving world of AI but also contribute to its growth and transformation.

Key Takeaways

- Strategic time management is key to fitting AI study into a busy life—use microlearning, productivity tools, and scheduled routines to stay consistent.

- Online AI courses (e.g., Coursera, IBM, DeepLearning.AI) offer flexible and scalable learning for both beginners and advanced learners.

- Staying updated requires regularly following AI news, academic research, and industry reports.

- AI communities and events (meetups, conferences, forums) offer networking and deeper engagement with the field.

Chapter 12

—

AI in Personal Development

F rom public speaking to mindfulness, AI is becoming a silent partner in personal growth. It listens, adapts, and coaches—providing feedback tailored to your voice, pace, and goals.

If you need to develop your soft skills or build confidence, AI can help you make meaningful progress faster.

AI as a Personal Coach: Enhancing Life Skills

Whether you're honing your negotiation tactics or perfecting your public speaking, AI tools provide insights and feedback, mirroring the support a personal coach would offer. These digital coaches analyze your performance, identify areas for improvement, and suggest actionable steps, making them indispensable allies in your personal growth. With AI, you can practice, receive feedback, and refine your skills, all from the comfort of your home.

AI tools cater to developing specific life skills by leveraging advanced algorithms to simulate real-world scenarios. Take, for instance, public speaking—a skill many find challenging yet essential in professional settings.

AI-powered platforms offer virtual environments where you can practice speeches, presentations, or pitches. These platforms use natural language processing to evaluate your delivery, offering feedback on pacing, clarity, and engagement. They highlight filler words, suggest pauses for emphasis, and even offer alternate phrasing to enhance your message.

Similarly, for negotiation skills, AI can simulate challenging discussions, providing a safe space to practice strategies and receive constructive feedback. This approach allows you to experiment with different tactics, growing more confident with each iteration.

Continuous improvement is a cornerstone of personal development, and AI excels in this area by tracking progress and providing real-time feedback. Consider an AI tool that records your practice sessions, analyzes your performance, and charts your growth over time. This data-driven approach allows you to visualize your development, identifying patterns and areas that require more focus.

Real-time feedback from AI not only highlights strengths but also pinpoints weaknesses, enabling targeted practice. This iterative process, supported by AI insights, fosters a cycle of continuous learning and enhancement, ensuring your skills evolve with each session. By integrating AI into your personal development routine, you create a dynamic feedback loop that accelerates your growth.

One of AI's most significant advantages is its ability to personalize coaching experiences, adapting to your unique learning style and preferences. AI tools can analyze your behavior, interactions, and responses to tailor feedback and suggestions that resonate with you. For instance, some learners thrive on detailed analytics and data-driven insights, while others prefer narrative feedback and practical examples.

AI adjusts its approach, ensuring that the coaching experience aligns with your cognitive style, maximizing engagement and retention. This personalization extends to the pace of learning, allowing you to progress at a speed that suits you, whether you're a fast learner or prefer a more gradual approach. By aligning with your individual needs, AI creates a supportive environment where learning feels natural and intuitive.

Mindfulness and Mental Health Apps Powered by AI

AI-powered mindfulness apps have become invaluable tools for those seeking mental balance in the chaos of everyday life. These apps are designed to guide you through meditation exercises, breathwork, and relaxation techniques, helping you cultivate a sense of peace and clarity.

By analyzing your engagement patterns, these tools tailor sessions to your needs, ensuring each experience is as effective as possible. Whether it's a five-minute breathing exercise to center yourself during a hectic day or a guided meditation to unwind before bed, these AI tools provide accessible and personalized support.

AI applications extend beyond mindfulness practices, playing a crucial role in mental health support. Virtual therapy sessions are growing in popularity, providing individuals access to mental health resources at their fingertips. These AI-driven platforms provide a range of services, from mood tracking and journaling prompts to cognitive behavioral therapy exercises. They create a space where users can explore their thoughts and emotions without judgment, offering immediate feedback and guidance.

This level of accessibility is particularly beneficial for those who may not have the means or opportunity to engage with traditional therapy. These tools enable individuals to take ownership of their mental well-being, fostering resilience and understanding.

The power of AI lies in its ability to collate and analyze data, providing insights that were previously unattainable. By monitoring user interactions, these apps can identify patterns and trends in behavior and mood. This data is then used to generate personalized recommendations, helping users understand their mental health better.

For example, an AI tool might notice that your mood dips on Tuesday afternoons and suggest a relaxation exercise or a short walk to boost your spirits. This level of personalization means that mental health support is no longer a one-size-fits-all solution. Instead, it becomes a dynamic and responsive experience tailored to your unique needs.

While the benefits of AI in mental health are profound, it's essential to address the ethical considerations and privacy concerns that accompany this technology. AI systems rely on great amounts of personal data in order to work effectively. This raises questions about data security and user privacy. It's crucial that developers implement robust security measures to protect sensitive information and that users remain informed about how their data is used.

Moreover, there's a need for transparency in how AI algorithms make decisions, ensuring that users understand the basis of the recommendations they receive. It's important to be aware of the limitations of AI tools, as they are not a substitute for professional mental health care. They should be seen as complementary resources that augment traditional support, not replace it.

In this digital age, AI-powered tools offer new ways to support mental health and mindfulness, making these practices more accessible and personalized than ever before. As you engage with these technologies, it's vital to remain mindful of both their benefits and limitations, ensuring that they serve as allies in your pursuit of well-being.

AI in Lifelong Learning and Self-Improvement

AI is at the forefront of the continuous learning revolution, transforming how we approach education and personal growth. Intelligent systems can understand your unique learning style, curating educational content that resonates with you. AI platforms assess your strengths and areas for improvement, then tailor lessons that match your pace and preferences.

Whether you best learn visually through hands-on activities, AI adapts, ensuring your educational journey is both engaging and effective. With AI, the barriers to learning diminish, making education a lifelong companion rather than a distant goal.

AI doesn't just make learning personal. It also helps you set and achieve personal development goals. Think of AI as a strategic partner in your quest for growth, offering tools that guide your progress in various areas. Want to learn a new language, develop a skill, or even delve into a new hobby? AI platforms provide structured plans, breaking down complex goals into manageable tasks. They track your progress, offering feedback that motivates and inspires.

This dynamic approach to goal setting ensures that you're not just dreaming of personal development but actively pursuing it. With AI, each step forward is clear and purposeful, turning aspirations into achievements.

The beauty of AI lies in its ability to seamlessly weave your learning plan into daily life. Learning doesn't have to be confined to a classroom or a specific schedule. AI facilitates ongoing skills acquisition, making it as natural as checking your phone or browsing the web. Imagine an app that delivers bite-sized lessons during your commute or a podcast that turns your workout into an educational session.

AI makes learning accessible and continuous, weaving it into the fabric of your everyday activities. This constant exposure to new information keeps your mind sharp and your skills relevant, ensuring that you're always ready for the next challenge.

A forward-looking, growth-centric mindset is crucial for continuous improvement, and AI plays a central role in fostering this mindset. By providing positive reinforcement and motivation, AI encourages you to embrace challenges and look at your setbacks as opportunities for growth. Personalized feedback helps you understand your progress, highlighting successes and guiding you through obstacles. This nurturing environment builds confidence, inspiring you to push your boundaries and explore new possibilities.

With AI as your ally, you learn to see the potential in every experience, cultivating resilience and adaptability. The journey of self-improvement becomes a rewarding adventure, filled with discoveries and achievements.

As you embrace lifelong learning, consider how AI can enhance your personal growth. Reflect on the skills you want to develop and explore the AI tools that can support your journey. By integrating AI into your learning routine, you open doors to new opportunities, enriching your life with knowledge and skills that empower you to thrive in an ever-changing world.

The Future of AI

Emerging technologies stand ready to redefine how we interact with machines, and among them, generative AI stands out. This technology enables machines to create content, from art to music, that rivals human creativity. It's not just about imitation. It's about inventing new patterns and exploring avenues that humans alone might not venture into.

Another promising field is quantum computing, which could exponentially increase the power of AI, solving complex problems incomprehensible with current computers. As these technologies mature, they promise to push the boundaries of what's possible, transforming industries and everyday life. The anticipation of these developments fuels excitement as we consider the potential applications and benefits they might bring.

While emerging technologies evolve, the pursuit of Artificial General Intelligence (AGI) continues to captivate scientists and philosophers alike. Unlike current AI, which excels at specific tasks, AGI aims to replicate the broad, adaptable intelligence seen in humans. The quest for AGI involves creating a machine that can learn, understand, and apply its knowledge across diverse domains, much like the human brain.

The implications of achieving AGI are profound, potentially leading to unprecedented advancements in science, medicine, and beyond. However, this pursuit also raises questions about the nature of consciousness and the ethical responsibilities of creating entities with human-like intelligence. The journey to AGI is fraught with challenges, requiring collaboration across disciplines to navigate the complexities of this ambitious goal.

As AI technologies advance, the potential for collaboration between humans and machines grows exponentially. In many fields, AI augments human capabilities, taking on tasks that require speed and precision, while humans provide context, creativity, and ethical oversight. Think of a surgeon in an operating room with AI-assisted robotic tools, where the machine's precision complements the surgeon's expertise and decision-making. This collaboration extends to creative fields as well, where AI assists artists in generating new ideas and pushing creative boundaries.

The synergy between human intuition and machine efficiency opens new possibilities, fostering innovation and problem-solving at unprecedented levels. As we embrace this partnership, we must consider how to balance efficiency with empathy, ensuring that technology serves humanity's best interests.

With the rise of AI, ethical dilemmas loom on the horizon, demanding careful consideration and proactive solutions. One pressing concern is bias in AI systems, which can perpetuate existing inequalities. As AI becomes more integrated into decision-making processes, ensuring fairness and accountability becomes paramount. There's also the challenge of data privacy, since AI systems rely on great amounts of personal data to function effectively. Protecting this data from misuse is crucial to maintaining trust.

Moreover, the potential for AI to replace jobs raises questions about the future of work and economic disparity. As these dilemmas unfold, society must engage in thoughtful discourse to establish ethical guidelines and regulatory frameworks that address these issues. Balancing innovation with responsibility will be crucial as we navigate the complexities of an AI-driven future.

Making AI Work for You: The Road Ahead

AI is not just a futuristic concept. It's a present-day tool that can significantly enhance your personal productivity and lifestyle. By automating routine tasks, AI allows you to focus on what truly matters. Whether it's sorting emails, setting reminders, or even optimizing your workflow, AI can handle it all.

The key is to integrate AI technologies that align with your daily habits and objectives. This integration won't just save time. It will also reduce the cognitive load, allowing you to channel your energy into creative and strategic activities. With AI taking care of the mundane, you can dedicate more time to innovation, personal growth, and leisure.

Adapting to an AI-driven world requires not only the willingness to adopt new tools but to effect a shift in mindset. It's about becoming more adaptable and making informed decisions. The landscape of work and life is evolving rapidly, and the ones who thrive will be those who can navigate this change with agility. Learn to leverage AI insights to make data-driven decisions.

For example, AI analytics can offer valuable insights into customer behavior if you're running a business, helping you tailor your strategies more effectively. On the personal front, AI can track your habits, providing feedback that leads to healthier choices.

Understanding how to interpret AI data and apply it meaningfully will be a critical skill. This adaptability, coupled with informed decision-making, will ensure you remain relevant in an ever-evolving environment.

Beyond personal productivity, AI has the potential to empower entire communities. Imagine a neighborhood where AI optimizes energy use, ensuring sustainability and reducing costs for everyone. Communities can harness AI for collective growth by implementing smart technologies that benefit the group. This could range from shared AI-driven transportation systems reducing traffic and pollution to community platforms that connect individuals with similar interests or needs.

Such applications not only improve quality of life but also foster a sense of unity and shared purpose. As communities increasingly adopt these technologies, they can address local challenges more effectively, from resource allocation to education and health services. This collective empowerment can lead to more resilient and thriving communities, capable of adapting to future challenges.

While AI presents many opportunities, we must remain vigilant about the risks. Ethical considerations, data privacy, and security must remain at the forefront of AI deployment. As individuals, staying informed about how your data is used and advocating for transparency in AI systems is essential.

Engage in discussions about AI's ethical implications and participate in shaping policies that govern its use. By being proactive and informed, you can help ensure that AI developments align with societal values and contribute positively to the greater good. Embracing AI with a balanced perspective will enable you to harness its potential safely and responsibly.

As we explore these themes, the road ahead is paved with possibilities. Embracing AI means opening doors to new efficiencies and opportunities, both individually and collectively. From personal productivity to community empowerment, AI offers tools that can transform lives. But as we navigate this landscape, we must do so thoughtfully, ensuring ethical considerations guide our path.

Key Takeaways

- AI serves as a personal coach, providing real-time, personalized feedback to help users develop skills like public speaking and negotiation.

- Mindfulness and mental health apps use AI to tailor experiences and provide support for well-being through exercises, journaling, and CBT-based prompts.

- Emerging AI technologies like generative AI, quantum computing, and the pursuit of AGI promise to expand personal and societal potential.

Conclusion

—

Writing Your Own Future

As we conclude this journey into the world of AI, I hope you now see this transformative technology in a new light. Throughout these pages, we've explored the fundamental concepts of AI, its practical applications, and the ways it can enhance your personal and professional life. From understanding the basics of machine learning to harnessing the power of AI-driven tools, you've gained powerful insights that can serve you well in this rapidly evolving landscape.

AI is more than just a buzzword. It's a force that is reshaping our world in profound ways. It's transforming industries, revolutionizing the way we work, and opening up new possibilities for growth and innovation.

As someone who has witnessed the disruptive power of technology firsthand in my own career, I can testify to the need to stay ahead of the curve. By embracing AI and understanding its potential, you position yourself to thrive in this new era.

But this book is not just about the grand, sweeping changes AI is bringing about in society. It's about empowering you, as an individual, to harness the power of AI in your own life. Whether you're a student, a professional, or simply someone with a curious mind, you now have the tools and knowledge to make AI work for you. From productivity apps to creative tools, AI is ready and able to help you reach your goals.

So, where do you go from here? The quest for learning and growth never ends, and I encourage you to keep exploring the fascinating world of AI. Engage with the resources and communities mentioned in this book, and don't hesitate to dive deeper into the topics that spark your interest. The more you learn, the more you'll discover the incredible ways AI can support and enhance your life.

As you integrate AI into your daily routines and work, remember to approach it with an open mind and a willingness to experiment. Not every tool or strategy will work for everyone, and that's okay. The key is to find what resonates with you and to keep refining your approach as you go. With time and practice, you'll develop a powerful AI toolkit that is uniquely tailored to your needs and goals.

It's important to remember that while AI is a tremendous asset, it's not a replacement for human ingenuity and creativity. As you leverage these tools, don't forget to bring your own unique perspective and skills to the table. The most powerful uses of AI are those that combine the efficiency of machines with the insight and imagination of the human mind.

As we look to the future, I'm filled with optimism about the potential for AI to create positive change in our lives and in the world. By embracing this technology and thoughtfully applying it, we can unlock new opportunities, solve complex problems, and build a brighter tomorrow. And with the knowledge and skills you've gained from this book, you are well-equipped to be a part of this exciting journey.

So, my friend, I invite you to step forward with confidence and curiosity. Explore, experiment, and discover all the ways AI can help you achieve your dreams. Share your experiences and insights with others, and be a part of the growing community of AI enthusiasts who are shaping the future.

Thank you for joining me on this quest for discovery and growth. It has been my privilege to share these experiences and discoveries with you, and I'm grateful for your trust and engagement. As you continue on your AI journey, know that you have the power to make a difference, both in your own life and in the world around you.

The future is bright, and with AI as your ally, the possibilities are endless. So go forth, embrace the power of AI, and create the life and career you've always dreamed of. The world is waiting for you to make your mark, and I can't wait to see what you'll achieve.

Glossary

Following is an abbreviated list of terms used throughout this book that are unique to the subject matter or used in a way—relative to AI—different from the meaning. Of course, no list can be exhaustive, so if you're ever in doubt, you can always ask ChatGPT or another language model what something means in context.

⁎⁎⁎

Accountability: The principle that developers and organizations should be responsible for the behavior and consequences of the AI systems they create.

Adaptability: The ability to adjust to new technologies, workflows, and job demands in response to a changing environment.

Adobe Sensei: Adobe's AI framework that powers advanced features like auto-tagging, intelligent cropping, and content-aware editing in creative tools.

Algorithm: A set of instructions or rules that a computer follows to solve a problem or complete a task.

Application Programming Interface (API): A set of protocols and tools that allows different software applications to communicate with each other.

Artificial General Intelligence (AGI):   A theoretical AI that possesses human-like cognitive abilities across diverse tasks and domains.

Artificial Intelligence (AI):   Technology that enables machines to perform tasks that typically require human intelligence, such as learning, decision-making, and problem-solving.

arXiv: An open-access archive where researchers upload preprints of scholarly papers in fields like computer science and AI.

Automation: The use of technology to perform tasks with minimal human intervention, often based on scheduled routines or learned behavior.

Bash/Zsh: Unix-based shell environments for macOS and Linux used in the terminal for scripting and command execution.

Bias (in AI): Systematic errors in AI outputs caused by prejudiced or unbalanced data used during training.

Black Box (in AI): A system whose internal workings are not transparent or easily understood by humans, making it difficult to trace decision-making.

California Consumer Privacy Act (CCPA): A California law giving consumers control over how businesses collect and use their personal data.

Canva: A user-friendly graphic design platform that uses AI to recommend design elements, layouts, and branding templates.

ChatGPT: An AI chatbot developed by OpenAI known for natural conversation and helpful responses across a wide range of topics.

Claude (model): A conversational LLM developed by Anthropic, focused on ethical alignment and user intent.

Cognitive Load: The total amount of mental effort being used in working memory; reducing it can improve focus and productivity.

Command Line: Another term for the terminal interface, used to execute commands directly without a graphical interface.

Community Empowerment: The use of AI to enhance collective well-being and collaboration within a group or neighborhood.

Confidence Threshold: A value indicating the minimum probability for a model to consider a detected object valid.

Content-Aware Fill: A feature that allows users to remove unwanted elements from images by automatically filling the space based on surrounding pixels.

Continuous Learning: The ongoing process of acquiring new knowledge and skills to stay current in a rapidly evolving field like AI.

DALL·E: An AI model by OpenAI that generates images from text prompts using diffusion-based methods.

Data Governance: The management of data availability, usability, integrity, and security to ensure trustworthy AI systems.

Data Preprocessing: The process of cleaning and transforming raw data into a usable format for analysis or training AI models.

Data Privacy: The protection and responsible use of personal data in AI systems to prevent misuse and ensure trust.

Data Visualization: The graphical representation of data to highlight patterns, trends, and insights using tools like Tableau or Power BI.

DeepL: A leading neural machine translation service known for its high accuracy, natural phrasing, and contextual understanding.

Dependencies: External libraries or packages that a program needs in order to run properly.

Diffusion Model: A type of generative model that creates images by gradually refining noise into coherent visuals.

Dynamic Computation Graphs: A feature of PyTorch that allows the network structure to be modified on-the-fly during execution, useful in AI research and prototyping.

ElevenLabs: An advanced AI audio tool focused on lifelike, emotionally nuanced speech synthesis, popular among creators and audio professionals.

Ethical AI: Practices that ensure fairness, accountability, and transparency in the development and deployment of artificial intelligence.

Explainable AI (XAI):   AI models and methods designed to make their decision-making processes understandable and transparent to humans.

Gemini (model): A Google-developed LLM designed for broad, multi-modal applications, including text, code, and more.

General Data Protection Regulation (GDPR):   A European Union law that regulates how organizations collect, store, and use personal data, granting individuals specific rights.

Generative AI: AI capable of creating original content such as text, art, music, or code, based on patterns learned from data.

Grammarly: An AI-powered writing assistant that provides real-time grammar, tone, and clarity suggestions.

Growth Mindset: A belief that abilities and intelligence can be developed through dedication and learning.

Hemingway App: A tool that analyzes text readability and highlights complex sentences, passive voice, and other stylistic issues.

Ideogram: A TTI model specialized in structured visuals like charts, diagrams, and educational graphics.

Intellectual Property (IP): Legal rights that protect creations of the mind, including patents, copyrights, trademarks, and trade secrets.

Large Language Model (LLM): A type of AI system trained on massive datasets of text to understand, generate, and respond in human-like language.

Latent Diffusion Model (LDM): A more efficient form of diffusion modeling that compresses images into a latent space before generating them. Used by Stable Diffusion.

Machine Learning: A branch of AI where systems learn from data and improve over time without being explicitly programmed for every scenario.

Make.com: A no-code platform for creating automations and connecting web apps and services.

Microlearning: An educational approach that delivers content in short, focused segments to support retention and fit into busy schedules.

Midjourney: An AI art generator known for highly stylized, artistic imagery, accessed via Discord.

Mistral: A high-speed, open-source LLM optimized for performance and real-time tasks.

Model Training: The process of feeding data into a machine learning algorithm so it can learn to make predictions or decisions.

Motion (application): An AI-powered task scheduling tool that dynamically arranges your calendar based on deadlines and shifting priorities.

Natural Language Processing (NLP): A field of AI focused on enabling computers to understand, interpret, and generate human language.

NaturalReader: A TTS platform known for its ease of use, wide range of voice options, and OCR capabilities that convert scanned documents into speech.

Neural Machine Translation (NMT): An advanced method of machine translation that uses deep learning and artificial neural networks to interpret and generate text.

Neural Network: A machine learning model inspired by the structure of the human brain, designed to recognize patterns and make decisions.

Notion (application): A popular productivity and note-taking platform that integrates calendars, databases, and AI-enhanced organization features.

Optical Character Recognition (OCR): A technology that converts images of text—such as scanned documents—into machine-readable formats for TTS or editing purposes.

OpenCV: A library for real-time computer vision tasks, often used in conjunction with AI for image and video processing.

Parameters (in AI models): The adjustable values within a neural network that are learned during training to improve performance.

Post-Processing: The editing or refinement of AI-generated images using external software like Photoshop or Canva.

PowerShell: A more advanced Windows command-line shell and scripting environment with greater flexibility than Command Prompt.

Pre-trained Model: An AI model that has already been trained on a large dataset, allowing it to perform tasks like detection without needing to be trained from scratch.

Productivity Dashboard: A central digital workspace that displays key tasks, data, and tools to help users manage their daily workflow efficiently.

Prompt: A user's input or question that initiates an AI response—can be a command, query, or creative scenario.

Prompt Engineering: The practice of crafting effective inputs to guide and improve AI outputs.

Public Domain: Creative works not protected by copyright that may be used freely by anyone.

Python (language): A popular high-level programming language widely used in AI and data science for its simplicity and extensive libraries.

PyTorch: An open-source machine learning framework developed by Meta, used for building and training deep learning models.

Quantum Computing: An emerging field that uses quantum-mechanical phenomena to perform computation, potentially boosting AI performance.

R (language): A programming language known for its statistical computing capabilities, commonly used in data analysis and visualization.

Real-Time Feedback: Immediate responses and suggestions provided by AI systems during practice or performance sessions.

Real-Time Object Detection: The process of identifying and classifying objects in video streams or images as they happen, often using pre-trained models.

Recommendation Engine: A system that analyzes past user behavior to suggest new content or products, commonly used in streaming and shopping apps.

Riffusion: A text-to-music tool that generates compositions in various styles by interpreting descriptive prompts through a neural network.

Right to Be Forgotten: A GDPR principle allowing individuals to request deletion of personal data under specific circumstances.

Saliency Map: A visualization technique used in AI to highlight which parts of input data (e.g., an image) most influenced the model's decision.

Self-Supervised Learning: A training method where AI learns patterns in data without explicit labels by predicting missing parts of the input.

Smart Home: A residence equipped with devices that automate tasks and can be controlled remotely via smartphone, voice commands, or automated scheduling.

Smart Speaker: A voice-activated device (like Amazon Echo or Google Home) that uses AI to perform tasks, answer questions, and control other smart devices.

Smart Thermostat: A device (e.g., Nest) that learns your temperature preferences and schedules, optimizing comfort and energy efficiency.

Speechify: A TTS app designed to help people with dyslexia and reading difficulties; it features voice customization and synchronized text highlighting.

Stable Diffusion: An open-source TTI model that runs efficiently on consumer hardware, allowing for community-driven customization.

STAR Method: A structured approach to answering behavioral interview questions by outlining the Situation, Task, Action, and Result.

Suno AI: A TTM platform that specializes in ambient and seamless audio loops, ideal for meditation, background soundtracks, or minimalist compositions.

TensorFlow: An open-source machine learning framework developed by Google, widely used for building and training deep learning models.

Terminal: A text-based interface used to interact with a computer's operating system by entering typed commands.

Terms of Service (ToS): A legal agreement between a service provider and a user outlining permitted usage, rights, and responsibilities.

Text-to-Image (TTI):   A category of AI models that generate images based on text descriptions or prompts.

Text-to-Music (TTM):   A creative AI process that generates music based on written prompts describing mood, genre, or emotional tone.

Text-to-Speech (TTS):   A type of AI technology that converts written text into spoken audio using natural-sounding synthetic voices.

Token: A piece of text (often a word or part of a word) used internally by language models to process and generate responses.

Traditional Programming: A method where a developer writes explicit rules for the computer to follow step by step.

Training Data: The dataset used to teach an AI system how to perform tasks by identifying patterns and associations.

Turing Test: A test proposed by Alan Turing to evaluate a machine's ability to exhibit behavior indistinguishable from a human in conversation.

Udio: An experimental TTM platform that produces avant-garde and unconventional music, encouraging artistic exploration.

Upskilling: The process of learning new skills or improving existing ones to stay relevant in a changing job market.

User-Generated Output: Content created by an AI in response to a user's input, typically owned by the user under most ToS agreements.

Virtual Assistant: AI software that responds to voice or text commands to help with tasks like reminders, navigation, and communication.

Virtual Private Network (VPN): A tool that masks a user's IP address and encrypts internet activity, improving privacy online.

Virtual Therapy: Digital mental health platforms using AI to deliver cognitive behavioral therapy, mood tracking, and journaling tools.

Windows Subsystem for Linux (WSL): A compatibility layer for running Linux command-line tools directly on Windows.

YOLOv5: A pre-trained deep learning model specialized in fast and accurate object detection in images or video.

References

The following references were used in researching the material in this book. Every effort has been made to credit original works, however if you identify parts of this work that reference materials not credited below, please notify us at permissions@adbooks.pub so we can correct any omissions.

*
**

AltexSoft. (n.d.). *AI image generation, explained*. Retrieved March 15, 2025, from https://www.altexsoft.com/blog/ai-image-generation/

AssemblyAI. (n.d.). *What AI music generators can do (and how they do it)*. Retrieved March 15, 2025, from https://www.assemblyai.com/blog/what-ai-music-generators-can-do-and-how-they-do-it/

Built In. (n.d.). *33 top artificial intelligence (AI) apps*. Retrieved March 15, 2025, from https://builtin.com/artificial-intelligence/ai-apps

CareerFoundry. (n.d.). *How to use ChatGPT: The full guide for beginners*. Retrieved March 15, 2025, from https://careerfoundry.com/en/blog/digital-marketing/how-to-use-chatgpt/

CBS News. (n.d.). *Your next job interview might be with AI. Here's how to ace it*. Retrieved March 15, 2025, from https://www.cbsnews.com/news/ai-job-interview-tips-to-prepare-artificial-intelligence/

CleanBrowsing. (n.d.). *Working with Windows Command Prompt and MacOS Terminal*. Retrieved March 15, 2025, from https://cleanbrowsing.org/help/docs/working-with-windows-command-prompt-and-macos-terminal/

Coursera. (n.d.). *Best AI courses & certificates [2025]*. Retrieved March 15, 2025, from https://www.coursera.org/courses?query=artificial%20intelligence

Daffodil Software. (n.d.). *20 uses of artificial intelligence in day-to-day life*. Retrieved March 15, 2025, from https://insights.daffodilsw.com/blog/20-uses-of-artificial-intelligence-in-day-to-day-life

DataCamp. (n.d.). *How to use DALL·E 3: Tips, examples, and features*. Retrieved March 15, 2025, from https://www.datacamp.com/tutorial/an-introduction-to-dalle3

Data Science Nexus. (n.d.). *25 ChatGPT prompts to supercharge your career growth*. Medium. Retrieved March 15, 2025, from https://medium.com/@datasciencenexus/25-chatgpt-prompts-to-supercharge-your-career-growth-7ddf9b00cf47

Datatron. (n.d.). *Real-life examples of discriminating artificial intelligence.* Retrieved March 15, 2025, from https://datatron.com/real-life-examples-of-discriminating-artificial-intelligence/

Dialzara. (n.d.). *CCPA vs GDPR: AI data privacy comparison*. Retrieved March 15, 2025, from https://dialzara.com/blog/ccpa-vs-gdpr-ai-data-privacy-comparison/

DigitalOcean. (n.d.). *14 AI design tools for creative professionals*. Retrieved March 15, 2025, from https://www.digitalocean.com/resources/articles/ai-design-tools

ElevenLabs. (n.d.). *Transform your text: Top 10 text-to-speech software for 2023*. Retrieved March 15, 2025, from https://elevenlabs.io/blog/transform-your-text-top-10-text-to-speech-software-for-2023

FastBots. (n.d.). *AI as a creative partner: Transforming modern art and design*. Retrieved March 15, 2025, from http://fastbots.ai/blog/ai-as-a-creative-partner-transforming-modern-art-and-design

Forbes Technology Council. (2025, January 10). *How artificial intelligence is transforming the job market: A guide to adaptation and career transformation*. Forbes. https://www.forbes.com/councils/forbestechcouncil/2025/01/10/how-artificial-intelligence-is-transforming-the-job-market-a-guide-to-adaptation-and-career-transformation/

IEEE Computer Society. (n.d.). *The rise of ethical concerns about AI content creation*. Retrieved March 15, 2025, from https://www.computer.org/publications/tech-news/trends/ethical-concerns-on-ai-content-creation/

Insightsoftware. (n.d.). *Traditional programming vs. machine learning*. Retrieved March 15, 2025, from https://insightsoftware.com/blog/machine-learning-vs-traditional-programming/

IOT on Main Street. (n.d.). *How AI enhances everyday life*. Retrieved March 15, 2025, from https://www.iotonmainst.com/how-ai-enhances-everyday-life/

Kelly, J. (2024, October 17). *5 top apps to improve time management in 2024.* Forbes. https://www.forbes.com/sites/jackkelly/2024/10/17/top-time-management-apps/

LegalNowAI. (n.d.). *Exploring AI tool terms of service: Beautiful.ai vs.* OpenAI. Retrieved March 15, 2025, from https://www.legalnowai.com/blog/exploring-ai-tool-terms-of-service-beautiful-ai-vs-openai/

LG Canada. (n.d.). *Benefits of artificial intelligence in your home.* Retrieved March 15, 2025, from https://www.lg.com/ca_en/connected-at-home/articles/benefits-of-ai-in-home/

Lumenova AI. (n.d.). *AI risk management: Transparency & accountability.* Retrieved March 15, 2025, from https://www.lumenova.ai/blog/ai-risk-management-importance-of-transparency-and-accountability/

Marr, B. (2023, July 5). *Debunking AI myths: The truth behind 5 common misconceptions.* Forbes. https://www.forbes.com/sites/bernardmarr/2023/07/05/debunking-ai-myths-the-truth-behind-5-common-misconceptions/

Maryville University. (n.d.). *AI vs. human intelligence.* Maryville Online. Retrieved March 15, 2025, from https://online.maryville.edu/blog/ai-vs-human-intelligence/

McKinsey & Company. (2023, August 1). *The state of AI in 2023: Generative AI's breakout year.* Retrieved March 15, 2025, from https://www.mckinsey.com/capabilities/quantumblack/our-insights/the-state-of-ai-in-2023-generative-ais-breakout-year

McNulty, N. (n.d.). *DALL·E vs. Midjourney vs. Stable Diffusion vs. FLUX.1: Comparing AI image generation tools.* Medium. Retrieved March 15, 2025, from https://medium.com/@niall.mcnulty/comparing-ai-image-generation-tools-DALL·E-vs-midjourney-vs-stable-diffusion-vs-flux-1-b394f95d36c4

Motion. (n.d.). *I tested 10+ AI personal assistants. Here are the best.* Retrieved March 15, 2025, from https://www.usemotion.com/blog/ai-personal-assistants

Motion. (n.d.). *We tested 50+ AI productivity tools. Here are the 16 best.* Retrieved March 15, 2025, from https://www.usemotion.com/blog/ai-productivity-tools

Nielsen Norman Group. (n.d.). *AI improves employee productivity by 66%.* Retrieved March 15, 2025, from https://www.nngroup.com/articles/ai-tools-productivity-gains/

Norton Rose Fulbright. (n.d.). *The interaction between intellectual property laws and AI: Opportunities and challenges.* Retrieved March 15, 2025, from https://www.nortonrosefulbright.com/en/knowledge/publications/c6d47e6f/the-interaction-between-intellectual-property-laws-and-ai-opportunities-and-challenges

Ozemio. (n.d.). *How AI is transforming organization with lifelong learning.* Retrieved March 15, 2025, from https://ozemio.com/blog/ai-and-lifelong-learning/

Perlow, J. (2023, August 28). *I've tested a lot of AI tools for work. These 4 actually help me get more done every day.* ZDNet. https://www.zdnet.com/article/ive-tested-a-lot-of-ai-tools-for-work-these-4-actually-help-me-get-more-done-every-day/

Python Central. (n.d.). *How to install PyTorch using pip: A step-by-step guide.* Retrieved March 15, 2025, from https://www.pythoncentral.io/how-to-install-pytorch-using-pip-a-step-by-step-guide/

Python Software Foundation. (n.d.). *BeginnersGuide/Download.* Python Wiki. Retrieved March 15, 2025, from https://wiki.python.org/moin/BeginnersGuide/Download

Rai, S., Mishra, D., & Mishra, A. (2023). *Interpreting black-box models: A review on explainable artificial intelligence (XAI).* Cognitive Computation. Advance online publication. https://doi.org/10.1007/s12559-023-10179-8

Restackio. (n.d.). *Best AI platforms for beginners 2025.* Retrieved March 15, 2025, from https://www.restack.io/p/beginners-guide-to-artificial-intelligence-answer-best-ai-platforms-for-beginners-2025-cat-ai

Sarun's Notes. (n.d.). *A comprehensive guide to text-to-video AI.* Retrieved March 15, 2025, from https://sarunnotes.com/a-comprehensive-guide-to-text-to-video-ai-the-next-revolution-in-content-creation-bb44558f51c4

Society for Human Resource Management (SHRM). (n.d.). *AI skills will be crucial for job seekers.* Retrieved March 15, 2025, from https://www.shrm.org/topics-tools/news/talent-acquisition/ai-skills-will-be-crucial-job-seekers

Stanford Institute for Human-Centered Artificial Intelligence. (n.d.). *AI index report*. Retrieved March 15, 2025, from https://hai.stanford.edu/research/ai-index-report

Towards Data Science. (n.d.). *Using AI to create new comic strips without writing any code*. Retrieved March 15, 2025, from https://towardsdatascience.com/using-ai-to-create-new-comic-strips-without-writing-any-code-cc669bb317a7

Ultralytics. (n.d.). *YOLOv5 quickstart*. Retrieved March 15, 2025, from https://docs.ultralytics.com/yolov5/quickstart_tutorial/

Wanyoike, M. (n.d.). *Building a strong AI portfolio: Showcase your skills to employers*. Medium. Retrieved March 15, 2025, from https://medium.com/muthoni-wanyoike/building-a-strong-ai-portfolio-showcase-your-skills-to-employers-d6be0c999f0a

Western Tidewater Community Services Board. (n.d.). *AI-powered mental health apps: Are they actually helpful?* Retrieved March 15, 2025, from https://www.wtcsb.org/ai-powered-mental-health-apps-are-they-actually-helpful/

Wikipedia. (n.d.). *List of large language models*. Retrieved March 15, 2025, from https://en.wikipedia.org/wiki/List_of_large_language_models

Zhou, L. (n.d.). *AI for coaches: 6 tools you need to learn now*. Retrieved March 15, 2025, from https://luisazhou.com/blog/ai-for-coaches

Keep the Conversation Alive

You've made it to the end—and now you have everything you need to take your first steps with AI, boost your productivity, and build a future-ready career.

That's something to be proud of.

Now it's your turn to help others find their way.

By sharing your honest thoughts about this book on Amazon, you're showing other curious minds—people just like you—where they can start their journey with AI.

Your review could be the signpost someone's been waiting for.

Because when we learn something new and pass it on, we keep the momentum going.

   —We keep the conversation alive.

      —We keep the spark lit for the next reader.

Thank you for being part of this movement. AI is changing the world—and thanks to you, more people will be ready for it.

To leave a review, just scan the QR code or follow this link:

https://www.amazon.com/review/review-your-purchases/?asin=1732755183

Together, we can make the future just a little brighter.

—Morgan Hale

Tempered Books

Built for thinkers, creators, and leaders to deliver cutting-edge insights in business, finance, and technology

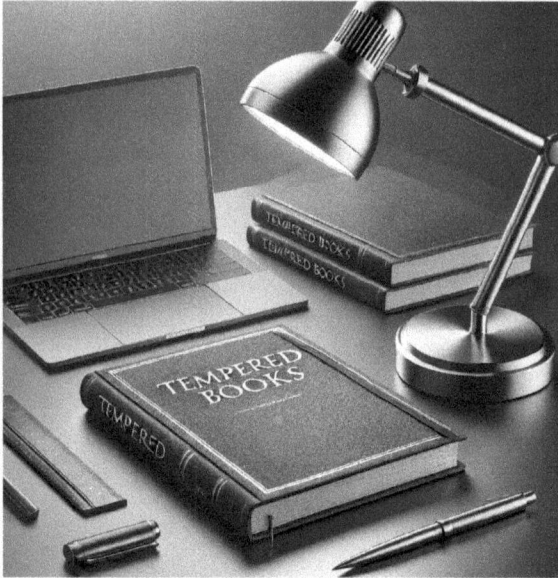

Whether you're building a business, sharpening your leadership skills, or rethinking how systems work—we're here to help you think clearly, act deliberately, and lead with purpose.

Explore more from Tempered Books and our sister imprints at: adbooks.pub

Download tools, templates, and bonus content from this book at:

adbooks.pub/resources

Questions, speaking inquiries, or media requests: info@adbooks.pub